SPLINTERS

from my

Rocking Chair

A JOURNEY THROUGH INCEST SURVIVAL

SPLINTERS

from my

Rocking Chair

A JOURNEY THROUGH INCEST SURVIVAL

Marcia J. Terpstra

authorHOUSE®

AuthorHouse™
1663 Liberty Drive
Bloomington, IN 47403
www.authorhouse.com
Phone: 1-800-839-8640

First published by AuthorHouse   09/13/2011

ISBN: 978-1-4634-3928-6 (sc)
ISBN:978-1-4634-3927-9 (ebk)

Library of Congress Control Number: 2011912771

Printed in the United States of America

I dedicate this book to sweet,

RACHEL

may IT be finished . . .

. . . may you see the LIGHT of day . . .

. . . may you find PEACE . . . !

May you forever be a whisper in the wind!

Whatever is done to you in the dark;
Tell it in the light!

Whatever is whispered in your ear;
Shout it from the rooftops!

The splinters in my soul are many. They have pricked at my very core since my mere existence. I was too young then to even understand that they were in me. I could not pluck them out. Some splinters grew into thorns and with every twist and turn they tore deeper into my soul. I began to bleed.

As I grew, I developed this keen sense of brokenness. I developed this constant state of longing; a nagging fear of decay. Nothing in my life made sense. I felt everything was my fault. I had to fix everything. I had this urgent need to justify my being, explain my existence and that I had worth and that I was lovable. Somewhere though, deep inside me, I somehow knew that my soul had a pulse, a pulse all its own. There was this whisper telling me so. This whisper was the only thing that kept me alive, that kept me moving. I was so confused.

Sadly, as time went on the cries won over the whispers. I stayed in a constant state of agony. I did not understand a thing. What was wrong with me! I just wanted to love and be loved. It seemed so simple. So why was I living this seemingly slow death. Why was it I could go through the motions of everyday life but really had not lived one moment at all? I was barely hanging on. I was raw with pain. I felt so empty. I just needed somebody to love me.

Why am I so alone? I feel so desperate. I need to be loved. I need you, whomever you are, to love me. I will give you every fabric of my being if you will simply love me. I will give you all I own if you would just love me. I will sacrifice my all for you. Just please touch me. Just please touch me with love. Just please hold me. Just please believe in me. Just please help me. What is wrong with me? Just hold me and hang unto me. Don't let me go!

Stop taking my flesh and walking away! Stop taking my flesh and leaving me to die!

My soul still bleeds and I am once again saturated with loneliness.

You see, I am an incest survivor and these are the splinters from my tiny little rocking chair.

THESE ARE THE SPLINTERS FROM MY ROCKING CHAIR!

SURVIVORS

We either live isolated ... or we live lost in a crowd.

Living in the middle ... there is no such thing.

INCEST

You snatched away that middle in me ...

SO I ROCKED!

AND ROCKED!

AND ROCKED!

AND ROCKED!

AND ROCKED!

!!!!!!!!!!!!!!!

!!!

SPLINTERS

The Chapters

SOUL

WHY WAS IT—OK

for you . . . to take your light from me;
for you . . . to leave me in darkness;
for you . . . not to nurture my soul;
for you . . . to be my shadow of death;
for you . . . to pluck yourself from me;
for you . . . not to see you were my all;
for you . . . to tear me to shreds;
for you . . . to rip right through me;
for you . . . to make me bleed;
for you . . . not to see I was dying;
for you . . . to leave me all alone;
for you . . . not to seek me out;
for you . . . to separate from me;
for you . . . to ignore my agony;
for you . . . not to see my desperation;
for you . . . to no longer love me;
for you . . . to stop the music;
for you . . . to hold back your passion;
for you . . . to take back your eternal love.

for you . . . why . . . why was it—ok . . .
for me . . . why . . . why was it—ok . . . to still love you.

HOW COULD I PERMIT THESE THINGS?

There was a third person in me; a tiny little child. I did not know what to do with her. I did not know how to care for her or how to grow her up.

I did not know how to tend to her cries.

I did not know how to hold her.

I did not know to feed her.

I did not know how to nurture her.

I did not know how to train her to walk.

I did not know how to give her wings.

I did not know how to help her.

I could not cradle her.

I did not know how to comfort her.

I could not give her a safe place.

I did not know how to shield her.

For I too, were just a mere child.

I loved her. I wanted to touch her. She stayed hidden in the shadows but I always knew she was there. I wanted her but I could never reach her. She eluded me.

She carried my soul with her. I wanted it back but I wanted her too.

I was splintered between her and me.

Who was the real one? Which one of us was the living and which one of us was the dead; most of the time, I did not know. Was she the shadow or was I?

I studied her so hard that I had no awareness of my own body; my own physical being. I did not want to acknowledge that existence of me.

I did my best to kill me, then maybe I could finally meet her.

Maybe I would finally meet her.

That little girl waiting in the wings for me!

BODY LANGUAGE

WHY WAS IT—OK

for you . . . to see I was rocking;
for you . . . not stop that rocking;
for you . . . to watch my banging;
for you . . . to let me bang my head;
for you . . . not to see my eating;
for you . . . to allow me to starve;
for you . . . not to see my blushing;
for you . . . not to ask why;
for you . . . to know I was sleepless;
for you . . . not to give me rest;
for you . . . to see I was anxious;
for you . . . not to calm my fears;
for you . . . to paint me red;
for you . . . color me black;
for you . . . not to see the color in me.

for you . . . why . . . why was it—ok . . .
for me . . . why . . . why was it—ok . . . to still love you . . .

HOW COULD I PERMIT THESE THINGS?

Rock-a-bye baby . . . rock, rock, and rockaway. I never had a cradle; I don't think. I only remember my rocking chair; that tiny little rocking chair. It was made of wood and slats of wood for a seat. I loved that chair but I grew out of it.

I found redemption in larger chairs. They were soft and they could even swivel. I could move in different directions now, while still rocking. I could rock and be held all at the same time, in the comfort of those cushions. I rocked and rocked for hours. No wonder I loved my rocking chair. It now held me in its arms.

I even rocked at bedtime. I had to leave my chair so I had to rock in yet another way. I curled up like a baby and rocked away. I was fetal in my stance and then I began to bang. Curled up in a ball, I banged my head against my bed's head board till I fell over. I banged my head in rhythm till I passed out. I was not even aware I had fell to sleep. I fell to sleep, so I slept.

When morning came banging at my door; the banging on that door frame, then the lighting of that room, somehow I got up and started all over again. I was taken from my rest; that mindless rest; not knowing that I was around, that I was living. I woke and went out into the world of my tiny little life, once again.

This became the pattern of my life. The banging. The door frame. This man in just his white underwear. His bulge. My fear.

I blushed. The surge of red and heat flooded my face. I could not stop it. Someone would spook me and I would blush. Someone would speak to me and I was red with shame. This began at the weaning of my rocking. I hated it. There was no privacy in it. The shame was now public knowledge. There was no escaping. The shame once personal was now public.

I knew I was deep red with confession. Shame yes, but maybe rage too; that rage. The rage I could not identify way back then. I only knew when I lived amongst others, I was so ashamed.

Embarrassment. Just a single word; just simply a polite word for those who have a moment of it. But I lived it each and every moment. I was so scared someone would spook me and I would have a rush of red. So I found another way to stay red in the face. This way it would be constant, it would be my color all of the time so if I blushed no one would notice. It became the color of me.

I struggled with putting anything into my mouth. I could barely feed me. It was not that there was no food. There was plenty of food. But when they ate, I could not eat with them. I wanted my own food, even if my own food was just simply a piece of toast. I wanted to be separate from them even if it meant I had to starve. I wanted no part of their feast. They did not love me so I did not want to share their food. I would rather go hungry than share food with those who were empty in their souls.

Once I had left that place, I had to begin the process of learning how to feed myself. It took baby steps. I could barely put hand to mouth with food. This was just the beginning; learning what to put in that spoon was another. I was on my own to feed myself.

If I could feed myself then maybe I could sleep. But there was nothing natural in sleeping. Sleeping was self induced. First it was the rocking, and then it became the alcohol. Sleep little child.

I waved an anthem that declared humans really need no sleep. It was a matter of the mind. If we used our minds they would keep us awake and safe from sleep. We had been brainwashed to believe we needed sleep. So I recruited others to join me in my unrest. It always ended with me alone.

I could not sleep, for I was on high alert. Even awake I was easily startled, how much greater would I be startled if I were sleeping.

If I dreamed it was only in nightmares. My dream world was that of tornadoes. My dreams were of being chased and falling down, unable to get up. My dreams were full of fear! My dreams were shear nightmares.

I flinched at every moment, every movement that I could not predict. I even flinched in love. You best not tap me on my shoulder. I would not be responsible once you did.

I grew to become excessively alert. I was aware of every movement around me. Nothing passed me by, not even the unintentional. I was keen. I was sharp to all of my surroundings.

I became a detective. I researched everything in my mind and sought answers. It was only in my mind though. I dare not act.

I knew others far more than they knew themselves, more than they could ever tell me; just by watching. Simply by watching them; but they never knew.

I dug into their dark looking for answers. I felt their dark and grieved to know why. I felt kindred to them. If only I could bring light into their darkness. I did for a while but I could not find the light in me.

I grew up scared of the dark; that black hole. I searched for answers and found none. There was no one to help me; only the dark. The dark still haunts me. I hated the dark. Why was I so afraid?

My heart pounded with fear every time there was a knock at the door. I prayed it was not for me. I remember hiding, waiting for someone else to answer. When I grew up and lived on my own, I knew that knocking was just for me and I hated it. Don't scare me or startle me. Don't come after me.

The ringing of the phone was just as fearful to me. I hated it. Who was calling? I hoped it wasn't for me! I prayed they did not want to speak with me. But as I grew and technology did to, caller ID gave me a fighting chance.

I learned at a very young age the longing to masturbate; the need for it. I was warned I might go blind should I perform this function; this physical need in me. Done right it was a spiritual blessing; an acknowledgment of my existence. And I can still see.

There were such smaller signs in me. I bit my inner cheeks as a child. I would relentlessly pick at my face.

I hated mirrors. I could not look me in the eyes, nor could I see any beauty in my face.

I would glance in the mirror only to see my flaws and pick at my imperfections.

I could not look in a mirror and stare me in the eyes; where my soul lied.

I would scratch at every scab on my body so any wound dare not to heal.

My bowels refused to work. When they finally did, I was in so much pain.

My urine flowed outside of my control; not in bed but in my school. They called them accidents. I mostly remember that one accident I had in my black and beige dress. I was sitting in my school desk and I poured all over me and unto the floor. It was a flood and there was no getting away from it. I had to run home.

Nothing was ever natural to me.
I hated my flesh!
For no one loved it; especially not me!

RELIGION

WHY WAS IT—OK

for you . . . to deny me my faith;
for you . . . to pray and not stay;
for you . . . not to love me;
for you . . . not to lend me mercy;
for you . . . not to give me grace;
for you . . . not to celebrate life;
for you . . . not to see I was precious;
for you . . . to have a law of your own;
for you . . . to judge me;
for you . . . not to give me love;
for you . . . to steal my joy;
for you . . . not to offer me peace;
for you . . . to not have patience with me;
for you . . . not to be kind to me;
for you . . . not to be faithful to me;
for you . . . not to be good to me;
for you . . . not to be gentle with me;
for you . . . not to have self-control;
for you . . . not to simply love me!

for you . . . why . . . why was it—ok . . .
for me . . . why . . . why was it—ok . . . to still love you . . .

HOW COULD I PERMIT THESE THINGS?

It was all a cover up. A cover up for the sins that lied behind closed doors, in the closets, and down in your basements. Nothing was truth, nothing was real. It was a land of make believe. It was a house of pretending.

Let's pretend all is well.

Let's pretend we are good.

Let's pretend we love.

Let's pretend to be joyful.

Let's pretend to be kind.

Let's pretend to be peacemakers.

Let's pretend we help each other.

Let's pretend we love one another.

If we look good on the outside, no one will dare look into our insides. We are in control. We are faithful to one God. This shall truly save us. There is no need to be faithful to no other but our God.

In God's name I will crucify, judge and condemn anyone who does not live up to MY commandments; for His name sake. I will shield and defend Him. I shall carry the sword for Him. I will cut down and chop off anything that gets in the way of my commandments.

You say, God help those who go against me. For they are the evil ones. They belong to him, the dark one. And I will shed no light on them. For they are his. Get thou behind me so you do not hinder me in my righteous walk. Lest I be tempted by your nature. Lest I have to reach down to help you up, or lest I be pulled down to you, or lest I maybe even fall down beneath you.

I was covered up with guilt, shame, blame. It began with the gentle act of incest then manifested into the fire and brimstone of religion. The incest seemed my greater friend.

As a child I truly loved God. The mere thought of Him gave me peace. He was my only peace.

I don't have much memory of my childhood but the most profound memory I have is the memory of that one Sunday afternoon, that warm summer day laying on a blanket under a shade tree and reading my little blue Bible. I can't tell you what I read; I can only tell you there was peace. It was God and I, not them. It was a sacred moment to me.

Then them . . . the judgment seat!

Each and every time I entrusted my nature to man, I was judged. I was so confused. The church acted one way and my God reached out to me in another. They were such hypocrites; so hateful, spewing hate, so I ran. I ran far, far away from them.

The only faith I took with me; was my faith I in their judgment of me. I had to flee from them.

I believed them, not Him. God did not love me. I was unworthy of God's love. So they told me so. Whatever happened to " . . . for the Bible tells me so . . ."??

I was cast out. I was no longer a part of them. I was on my own. God no longer wanted me. According to them I was without God. According to them I was demon possessed.

The only demon that ever possessed me was their lack of love for me; that was all!

Hypocrites!

I could not bask in the light because of them. They kept me in the dark. They kept me in secret; behind closed doors, in the closet, in dark basements. I screamed to let my little light shine. I would be locked up if I dare do so.

I was raised in a church that had so much condemnation for the outside world. Salvation was not available for any of the rest of humanity outside our walls; including other churches. The only ones to be saved were the church goers on that one street, on that one corner of that one block, those inside that one building, that one sanctuary; no one else would be spared.

The haunting began; once in this sanctuary, (funny, how they call these places sanctuaries). I had to look over my shoulder.

Who else within these walls might be next to be condemned; to be condemned to hell? This was the house of hate. I kept looking over my shoulder! Might I be next; may it be me?

I ran like hell from all of it. I did not want to be the first one taken nor the last one standing there.

I ran and fought to find my own way. I hated I had been so deceived. All their sins had been covered up so they were as pure as the driven snow. Me? I questioned them and challenged them over their so called God given authority.

There is no authority in love; only love. Love has no rights and wrongs. It crosses all divides. You trust love to heal all things, to mend all wounds. Love loves unconditionally. Love is mightier than the sword. Love does not judge. LOVE is as great to perfection as one can get.

Those I loved most, I was most betrayed by. I was led to the wilderness to fend for myself. I did not do well. There was no love around me. There was no love on either side, neither the side of the righteous nor the side of the world. I was stuck.

I hid my agony in the animal world. I became Christ like there.

I became the good shepherd. I watched over "my sheep". Like a shepherd in the field, you have no voice other than to call your sheep. So I lived in silence. I spoke only to them, "my sheep". I would feed "my sheep". I would call them all by name. I prayed over them each time I would have to leave them; "I love you angels. God bless you. God bless this house and all you creatures in it. I will see you tonight—God willing. I love you".

If only I had been so loved. If only I could have been a sheep to that Good Shepherd!

I could never hear the whispers of God for the shouting of evil men.

I learned ever so young to remain silent. I learned so young that I should remain in the basement of incest; deceit, secrecy. As I grew older, I was to remain in the halls of that sanctuary, walls of that basement. "You are to remain silent . . ." Isn't that what they say before they take you in?

Religion taught me it was ok to violate those you love so long as you go to church on Sunday. I saw Sundays as a special day for the wicked; getting away with murder through the week. And now on the Sabbath, claiming the throne of the righteous, sitting in your judgment seat with the wrath of God in you!

You used weapons against me; you perverts, you abusers, you liars, you cheaters, you killers of God's creatures, you child molesters . . . I had no weapon to use against you for I was just a child. The weapon you used against me was The Word.

You twist and turn things.

Later in life I saw your churches use the Word, according to you, for better offerings and greater congregations. Greed—the greed of money and the greed of gathering the masses. It all looked good. But it had nothing to do with caring for the humble, the broken.

And you preachers, where are your sermons on that darker side other than me? Where were your sermons against you? Where were your sermons against the sins you committed? Where were your sermons against even the greater sins?

Where are your sermons against incest?

Where are sermons against child abuse?

Where are your sermons against abuse of any kind?

Where are your sermons against pornography?

Where are you sermons against neglect?

Where are all these sermons, you so called preachers???

You preachers of light.

You teachers of darkness.

You preachers of love.

You teachers of hate.

You preachers of the Word, you hearers of the Word, but not doers of the Word.

Why can't you preach about the sins you commit. SAY IT!!! SAY IT!!! Say it you preachers. Say it you teachers. SAY IT!!! SAY IT!!! SAY IT!!! You must tell your children. Help them in the truth.

Truth is not judgment. Truth is the healer of all things. Truth is the surrender of all secrets. TRUTH is the bridge to every injustice.

SAY IT!!! SAY IT!!! SAY IT!!! Take your lies from your Sunday mornings. Take your lies from your pulpits. Get in the basement with me and show me your love. Show me there is something worth crawling out for. Take the rock from my tomb. Show me a beacon. Help me!

I cry in the dark, waiting; waiting for the righteous to save me. Faith, hope, love—these three . . . none of these were given to me.

Father, Son and Holy Ghost—the Trinity I believed in. Hate, Rejection and Judgment—the trinity that surrounded me.

How dare you take my precious Jesus from me and nail me to a cross. For His will was not done!

Careful how you teach your children!

SHAME

WHY WAS IT—OK

for you . . . to ridicule me;
for you . . . to criticize me;
for you . . . to speak crossly to me;
for you . . . to talk down to me;
for you . . . to put me down;
for you . . . to shame me;
for you . . . to say I deserved it;
for you . . . to steal my dignity;
for you . . . to insult my integrity;
for you . . . to deny my successes;
for you . . . to take my deserving from me;
for you . . . to think my time has no meaning;
for you . . . not to believe I mattered;
for you . . . to focus on my failures;
for you . . . to dwell on my errors;
for you . . . to blame it all on me;
for you . . . not to look at yourself;
for you . . . to blame only me;
for you . . . to make me feel guilty;
for you . . . to put me to shame.

for you . . . why . . . why was it—ok . . .
for me . . . why . . . why was it—ok . . . to still love you . . .

HOW COULD I PERMIT THESE THINGS?

It was written all over my face.

Every dirty little secret. My shame and all of their sins too.

I was damaged goods and they knew it. The only difference was they could go on. I could not. They seemed to revive from theirs; resurrect themselves. But I had no saving of my own. I was ashamed to live—knowing.

My thoughts embarrassed; shamed me. I was to blame. They were my thoughts. I did not birth them on my own. I believed in love and this was the only love I knew. The dark love. The secret love. The hidden love. The love in the basement; dark. I was ashamed and I felt dirty. I kept looking for life. I could write of my childhood; if only I remembered having one.

I remember falling off my bike, into that pricker bush.

I remember playing behind the tracks, mostly by myself.

I remember delivering the Grit every Saturday on my red sting ray.

I remember the muck farms and the pennies I made.

I remember feeling destitute while sorting those radishes and planting those onions.

I remember Princess, Coronal and Rusty; pets along the way.

I remember the cold of winter; when there was no thawing.

I remember being held by my grandfather as my family drove away.

I remember pulling dandelions; only to be stung by a bee.

I remember laying under that tree with my Bible; at peace.

I remember getting up at four am to babysit while on summer vacation.

I remember that toothache that lasted for months.

I remember listening to Children's Bible Hour and those Billie Graham Crusades.

I remember my Barbie doll. I hated that Ken, when he came along.

I remember those JC Penny catalogs and yes, Sears too. My favorite section had nothing to do with toys and the things that children dream of. I would feast on the pages of those who had little clothes.

I remember going to church every Sunday; twice.

I remember some parts in the basement with him.

I remember enough of it.

I don't really have many fond memories of my childhood. Everything just seemed to be heartache. There was nothing normal about me; nothing seemed natural. The greatest excitement I had as a child was only in my fantasies.

I didn't play with Barbie and Ken like a normal child would. I had my own way of playing with them, mostly Barbie. I had lots of fantasies. I knew these dolls darker sides; their secret desires. I played it out for them.

I was mad when they introduced Ken. Barbie and I were having such a good time. I did not want him. I hated when they brought him in; him and his bulge. He ruined my fantasies, my life.

I somehow knew I was nowhere near a normal child.

You see, there was nothing at all normal about me as a child. I saw everything through the lenses of sexuality. There were no rose colored glasses, only dark with dirt. I could not figure out what was wrong with me. Sex was normal so what was not???

After that first basement was empty, I sought another. It was the neighbor boy. I still really don't know if he sought me or if I sought him. I only know the results were the same only better for him. I got real good at it. I mastered it. I went downstairs to be with him every chance he gave me; so many, many times and for many years. He was such a lucky boy.

As he grew into a man, he let me go, pushed me away. By then it was too late for me. I trusted no man. I learned boys only wanted one thing and I grew to believe that men to only did too.

But I remained determined to be loved so I pressed on. I gave them everything they asked for and even more. Men loved me like that. Certainly this would insure true love for me!

Where the heck did I get this thinking? The first did not stay with me. And not even the neighbor boy. Where did I ever get that anyone else would? I kept trying.

I had a few dates with this one man. He was different. We saw the movie together; "A Star is Born". At the end of the date when I tried what I knew, it was all over. This was foreign to me. I did not get this. I could have fallen madly in love with this one. I guess it was ok though; for I preferred Barbie's anyway.

No matter how hard I worked, nothing brought me love. I felt filthy in my efforts. I blamed myself for all that went wrong. Yet I didn't even know what was right. I was a mere child when it all began. That dark, cold basement!

And then there was guilt!

This was the closest I ever came to being one of them, one with the religious. We were one because of our guilt. Our kinship was in the guilt of our everyday sins.

I was all alone in the guilt of that one major sin committed against me. I alone owned this one.

There was no shame in their crimes of incest, only a cover-up.

I shaved my head once, even twice in shame only to say "See, see, I gave you what you wanted. Here is proof; proof of my shame. Here is my standing naked before you. See! See!" What more can I do to show you I am not worthy of you!

I walked on like an ape. I walked through life dragging my knuckles to the ground, bending my shoulders, holding my head down in shame.

Guilty to be alive!

HOPELESSNESS

WHY WAS IT—OK

for you . . . to say I was unworthy of your love;
for you . . . to proclaim I was too damaged;
for you . . . not to help me;
for you . . . to carve at my heart;
for you . . . not to acknowledge my pain;
for you . . . to confine me below;
for you . . . to trap me;
for you . . . to deny me my joy;
for you . . . to mock my brokenness;
for you . . . to shake my beliefs;
for you . . . to loosen my strengths;
for you . . . to ignore me;
for you . . . not to heed to my pleas;
for you . . . not to be grateful for me;
for you . . . to make fun of my efforts.

for you . . . why . . . why was it—ok . . .
for me . . . why . . . why was it—ok . . . to still love you . . .

HOW COULD I PERMIT THESE THINGS?

I saw this girl . . . the rest of the day didn't matter. She was maybe six or seven. I don't know. I do not know time or ages; I can't even remember dates. I only know the emotional stamp that was left in me.

There is no age to anything, only a remembrance.

I saw this girl in this Good Will store. She caught my eye. She had beautiful long blond hair. She was at the side of whomever she belonged to, yet she seemed to belong to no one at all. She seemed to be afraid, as if she wanted to cover herself. She posed quietly, skillfully; some moments with her arms down but mostly with her hands curled under her chin. She seemed shy, even shameful.

I caught a glimpse of her face. I had to look again to see if it were not me. This beautiful little girl was all alone. I had to look twice to be sure it wasn't me. I saw pain in this little girl. She seemed so invisible.

I was invisible. I was always looking out with no one looking in; with no one looking back at me. I attempted to live in life but there was no one watching me. There was no one watching over me. No one protected me; no one shielding me. I had no safe place nor did I ever have solid ground to stand on. There was no such thing as security.

I lived my life through a looking glass—detached; detached from the land of the living; detached from the land of the dead. I was invisible.

I developed my own philosophy on hope. I defined hope as a mirage in the dessert; in that seething heat. Hope was this wavy, tempting illusion. Each time you get close, it disappears. It gets snatched from you just as you believe it is real; just as you reach out to touch it, and then it is gone. Hope eludes you. Hope is a tease, a mirage. Hope keeps you chasing for things that will never be. This was my definition of hope.

I passed on the mirages yet I remained in the dessert with no direction. Lost, hungry, thirsty and tired. I felt I would wander all my life with no relief. I might live or I would die.

I mustered the strength to build a fortress. I had to in order to protect what little was left of me. Sadly, each time I took a mere step outside my walls, there it was again. The rejection, the abandonment, the judgment of me, the loneliness, that hate—it was all still there, greater than life. Just yet another fatal blow to myself by trusting in them.

The exposing of me always led to my death. I taught myself the fine art of running and the fine art of hiding. Kind of like the children's game of hide and seek only no one was seeking me. No one really cared for me, cared to seek what was in me.

Maybe I did not want to be found; just maybe. Maybe, being found for however briefly, meant a hiding in deeper corners; corners like in that basement I was so familiar with. I made that place my home. It was familiar to me. It was my resting place. At least I was there; the IT that BECAME me.

I waited not daring to move. I performed outside of myself. When it was done I hated me and loved him. I longed and ached for him to love me back. I associated his love for me in my performance to him. He would love me if I gratified him. He would "love" me within the corners of that basement, but outside those walls there was no love for me.

I would sink into nothingness and fade away. It was kind of like quick sand. I would step out and slip in. I would take one more step and it was over. I was pulled down and sucked under. I was swallowed up and devoured. Like quick sand it was a slow agonizing suffocation of me.

I walked on eggshells. I felt paranoid so much of the time. I felt paralyzed. I did not dare move; for if I moved it meant disruption of things around me, maybe even destruction. Like dominoes, if I moved everything around me would fall down.

Fault followed me everywhere. I dare not touch the children lest I be accused of things other than genuine love. Touch is a very cautious thing to many in the light of day. But there is little concern for the touching of children that goes on in the dark when no one is watching. There was no escape.

I tried desperately to live. I did so many external things to revive me; to bring life in me; to pull me out. No matter how hard I tried or no matter what I tried I could never get a sense of belonging.

To the outside world, many would say I have lived a full life. I have seen many places, done many different things and fought many causes. I have gone into areas that many would not dare to venture. But I never belonged to anyone or any one place. I did magnificent things and conquered much but I never belonged at all. Some might even be envious of my so called life; that life that they could see.

I fought for everyone's life; everyone's life but my own.
I fought for everything other than me!
I fought for anyone besides me!

ABANDONMENT

WHY WAS IT—OK

for you . . . to reject me;
for you . . . to cast me out;
for you . . . to take yourself from me;
for you . . . not to share with me;
for you . . . to stop building together;
for you . . . to devalue what mattered to me;
for you . . . to turn me down;
for you . . . to turn your listening ear;
for you . . . not to hear my cries;
for you . . . to reject my desires;
for you . . . not to pay attention;
for you . . . to give me just memories;
for you . . . not to stay with me;
for you . . . to give up on me;
for you . . . to turn my truth against me;
for you . . . to say I don't count;
for you . . . not to admit your cruelty;
for you . . . to sit back and do nothing;
for you . . . not to help me;
for you . . . to toss me to the side;
for you . . . to ignore my ideals;
for you . . . to argue my input;
for you . . . to dispute my opinion;
for you . . . to give up on us;
for you . . . to throw dirt on me;
for you . . . to isolate me;

for you . . . to stonewall me;
for you . . . to be so cold;
for you . . . not to mourn my losses;
for you . . . to dislike my likes;
for you . . . to neglect me;
for you . . . to diminish my worth;
for you . . . to lay me to waste;
for you . . . not to believe in me;
for you . . . to leave me.

for you . . . why . . . why was it—ok . . .
for me . . . why . . . why was it—ok . . . to still love you . . .

HOW COULD I PERMIT THESE THINGS?

"Jesus loves me this I know."??? Too bad they didn't. If only they had!

They are void of any loving-kindness. Theirs was a heart of steel, cold and unbending. Solid as a rock. There was no penetrating. I rolled off them as water rolls off oil. Their hearts were frozen, a glacier of ice. Not even the sun could melt them. So how dare I.

I was their sacrificial lamb. Put her away. Burn her at the stake. Silence this voice. She is too aware for us. She is alert and ready. She must go. There must be no evidence of her. "Vanish her, I say!"

I had to run. I had to hide. I guess I gave them what they wanted. I surrendered and sacrificed myself. I would not let them do it to me so I did it to myself. I did not stay and fight. It was a losing battle. I could stay and be torn to shreds or I could go and slowly die. I chose the latter.

Being alone was my protection. Being alone shielded me from them, all of them. They could not hate me if I was not there. I was rejected by all of them; family, friends, the church, and by God according to them. And I believed them.

I even had an employer tell me that if I did not go back to church I would lose my job. That is Christ-like isn't it? You hearers, not doers. Why would I want to belong?

I had to save myself. I did not do a very good job of this. I kept getting involved with people just like me; the wounded, the rejected, the abandoned. We could barely save each other; couldn't. There was no other choice but to leave each other. We had to abandon one another so we might have had one more chance to survive.

As I look back on all of us; the wounded, the rejected, the abandoned; we had one common thread. We all were raised to believe in God. This still puzzles me. What a parody!

How could you play God with our lives? Where was your love? How could we ever believe?

I proclaimed for many years that I would rather walk the streets alone, homeless, than to go back there, back there to give them yet another chance to forsake me. I refused to go home. Staying away, they could not lock me up nor confine me. I stayed far from them; for away from them I felt safe.

I was miles away. They did not want me with them so what really did it matter.

I to this day do not understand their hate, their rejection, their forcing me to flee, their abandonment of me. It was haunting.

I was a good person. I was kind. I was loving. I was fair. I was attentive. I cared. I shared. I had compassion. I could reason. I was serving. I was gentle. I was good to all. I did my best anyway.

To those I loved and knew? I watered them as flowers in my garden. I loved each and every one of them even as they wilted from me.

My goodness mattered nothing to them. They hid behind their praise of me. They were only words. They were only words so I would honor them.

It was all about them. They never took the time to know me. The only caring they had was my caring for them. That's all. It had nothing to do with me.

A time or two I came close to someone caring for me but in the end I was left behind; neglected and alone.

No one ever stood up for me. No one ever stayed. My heart ached; my soul ached. I clung to simple acts of kindness towards me and to those that seemed to need me; believing, trusting. None of it was real or true.

They all fired a flame in me in the beginning. In the end, I was left with only ashes. I was a part of nothing. I was a part of no one. I have evidence. For they are all gone!

Ashes to ashes.

Why would they not touch me!
Why?
Why could they not love me and stay!

DEPRESSION

WHY WAS IT—OK

for you . . . to keep me inside;
for you . . . not to play with me;
for you . . . to cater to your own desires;
for you . . . not to tend to my needs;
for you . . . not to lift me up;
for you . . . not to respect my being;
for you . . . to let me fade away;
for you . . . not to see I was lost in you;
for you . . . to take my identity;
for you . . . not to see I still existed.

for you . . . why . . . why was it—ok . . .
for me . . . why . . . why was it—ok . . . to still love you . . .

HOW COULD I PERMIT THESE THINGS?

My life was an open wound. Nothing would ever heal. There were layers upon layers of infestation. Layers upon layers of abuse. It all began the day of my incest.

I lived each day in anguish. There were no flowers in my world; only twisted vines. Their roots were deep in me. I was so empty. I was so sad. I was so anxious. I was desolate. I was scared. I was all alone. I was so afraid. Each day I wanted to run but I didn't know why. Where would I run to? There was no safe place. I wanted to bury myself and hide.

Each time I raised my head to come out of the ground and dare live, more dirt got shoveled in my face. Everything seemed hopeless. I could barely take care of myself. I could barely survive.

Earth was my hell. I knew from birth, there was no life here; only my breathing. I wish I never took that first breath. Taking that first breathe is what got me here to begin with. It is what trapped me; trapped here on this earth.

Why was I here anyway? There was destruction everywhere I went; destruction within me and destruction around me. Destruction consumed me; destruction consumed the world around me.

I remain here against my wanting. I never really belonged here. Not at my birth, not in that basement. Why did I get out at birth! Why could I not get out of that basement?

I tried so hard to revive myself. I fought so hard to belong, to belong somewhere; to belong anywhere. I strived to belong with family, I strived to belong with friends, I strived to belong in sports, I strived to belong in churches, I strived to belong in clubs, I strived to belong in relationships, I strived to belong in bed, I strived to belong in bars, I strived to belong in causes, I strived to belong. Despite it all, nothing remained. I belonged to nothing.

I could hear silent screams in the dark.

I died little by little each and every day. I did not die just once in that womb. I did not die just once in that basement. I did not die just once in that rocking chair. But I died over and over again each and every day. I never fit into my own being. I never fit into my own existence.

I am half way to dead. I dare not to dream. I was as a dog on a chain; no food, no water and nowhere to roam.

If I had been a bird, I then could fly.

I lived my life on deaths door, some may call it death row. I lived in the shadow of silence. I hated each step. Moving forward in my shackles was so uncertain. Moving backwards, well . . . I could only rock.

If only I were a bird!!!

The grains of time slipped through my hands. Dust to dust; I could hardly wait!

I confessed my faith when I was young. I think it was called "Profession of Faith". It was after my grandfather committed suicide. Yet another testimony of hopelessness; darkness clings to darkness I guess. Yet another silent scream in the dark. The dark wins yet again.

I truly did feel my Jesus in me, and my Lord too. But that was in me. Outside of me there was no celebration. My Profession of Faith seemed to be more about your bending of my arm rather than a celebration of what was in me. It was a carnal surrendering; so I would become part of your flock.

It had nothing to do with me!

It had nothing to do with my God in me; oh, yes He was there. For I knew the day was at hand that I would soon be cast out despite my Profession of Faith. I knew my days were numbered.

I was so broken. I was so torn. Your lives seemed so perfect. What was wrong with me? Life seemed so easy to you. Although I sensed you needed to cry. I wanted to cry too, all the time. I lived pain to pain; you seemed to live glory to glory or so the world would see.

My entire story was that of pain. They had no story at all. They could not, nor dare not tell theirs.

Beneath my pain, I somehow knew I was good; I somehow knew I only wanted to love. I patiently waited as strangers told me their stories. And when they were done I would encourage them and build them up. How could that be bad? I tried to fill just a portion of their empty holes if even for a moment. I felt for them, these strangers. And they attached to me, if only but a moment.

I was not white washed as you. I was stained and damaged. The bones in my soul were broken. The bones of your soul were dead.

I wanted no part of being a framework to despair. I wanted no part of being a framework to loneliness. I wanted no part of being a framework to rejection. I wanted no part of being a framework to abandonment. I wanted no part of any of it.

I loved them all, not just strangers but even the near and dear. So what was wrong with me, that no one loved me!

If not a bird, a butterfly! After all, I had been a caterpillar all my life, crawling.

I now live in a cocoon; so why not one day to be a butterfly? Why not, why not me to be a butterfly?

Maybe I could just flutter and be.

Maybe I was not meant to fly.

Maybe soaring is just for the birds!

Soaring takes a force of one's own. Soaring takes the wings of one's own being. But I had no wings! I had plenty of feet to crawl. But where were my wings?

My God; my God, where are you?!!!

Time stands still for people like me!

LONELINESS

WHY WAS IT—OK

for you . . . to no longer want me;
for you . . . to leave me all alone;
for you . . . not to see my sadness;
for you . . . to take your heart from me;
for you . . . to no longer feel my love;
for you . . . not to get my hurting;
for you . . . to withhold from me;
for you . . . to take back your love;
for you . . . to hide your heart;
for you . . . to exclude me;
for you . . . to pretend I don't exist;
for you . . . to make me invisible;
for you . . . not to validate me;
for you . . . not to acknowledge me;
for you . . . not to recognize my contributions;
for you . . . to ignore my passion for your life;
for you . . . to be blind to my sacrifices;
for you . . . to deny my participation;
for you . . . to leave me hungry;
for you . . . not to eat at my table;
for you . . . to leave me so empty;
for you . . . to leave me stranded;
for you . . . to forget my love for you.

for you . . . why . . . why was it—ok . . .
for me . . . why . . . why was it—ok . . . to still love you . . .

HOW CAN I PERMIT THESE THINGS?

Happy Holidays!

I have spent most every one of them alone. The holidays came, the holidays went; each of them, just as any other day.

I worked to make these days festive though for just me; each holiday that I was alone. I would prepare a feast for me; just me; only me. I prepared the foods of my choosing and the preparation of them seemed even fun. There was no one to get in my way. But when I sat to eat the fruits of my labor, then, then I truly understood how desperately lonely I was. There was this profound sense of being alone.

Oh, how I deceived myself.

Yes, I had some years of so called togetherness. Yes, I have had several commitments for a lifetime. But they are all gone. Life, reality, hardship, selfishness; mostly their selfishness, ended them all.

I did not know which was worse; to live a life of loneliness longing for the love of your life or to live a lifetime with someone who never really loved you. I almost had both.

I was a servant to every one of those who claimed to love me. I left myself behind just to be with them. Just as I was taught from IT. I only knew the serving kind of love; I learned it in my innocence. I chose those who only desired to be served; or did they choose me?

Inside myself, I prayed, I ached, I longed for, I would die for that one person to come into my life and love me; that one person who wanted to know me and never leave me. I was in agony.

I sought after from afar. I wanted to be desired.

I wanted to be sought after as he had sought me in that basement. But then he was gone. So too my life since then. I was sought after; I served them and then they were gone. I was then left behind yet again.

If only one person would see my soul, and stay. Touch me and stay. Stay by my side each and every day. Lay by my side each and every night. I know now that my only everlasting would be my everlasting loneliness.

Love had eluded me. So mostly through my life I have lived alone. I lived alone in the privacy of mine own actions. I lived alone in the privacy of my own mind. I lived alone in the privacy of my own heart. I lived in the privacy of my own spirit. I lived in the privacy of mine own soul. It was not my choosing. There was no other choice.

I can't begin to tell you how extremely difficult this was; to prosper all alone. To prosper not for the long run with someone at your side to fill the gaps, but to prosper day in and day out all on my own. It took all I had. It took my every fiber. Just to survive, alone. I had to fight alone just to live; just to keep breathing.

Fighting alone was one thing; loneliness is such a different thing. They are almost polar opposites. Aloneness welcomed me. Loneliness haunted me. Aloneness freed me. Loneliness never let go of me.

Even as a child, loneliness and sadness went with me where ever I went. Loneliness and sadness walked hand in hand with me, always; everywhere I went.

I had a saving grace along the way in my life; but for a brief time. I was sincerely blessed with a circle of loving friends while in high school. We laughed and played a lot together; as children do. I felt like a child for the first time in my life. I belonged.

These were the only true moments of love that I had ever felt. I loved them dearly. But something was wrong within me. I was unworthy of them. How dare I be loved? I was embarrassed at the thought of being loved. I felt ashamed. Being loved was not my deserving.

I felt so ashamed to love them back. And it showed. It showed on my face each time they spoke to me. I was ashamed to love them. I would turn red with unworthiness when they focused on me. I was flooded with shame and a fierce blushing would come over me. I was filled with shame because they loved me. I was filled with shame because I loved them back.

I had a touch of heaven but for a while; for they just simply loved me.

Those days are long gone—evaporated through time. But their love will live forever in me.

We had to part. I went off away from their love. I had to grow up now, alone.

Go away little girl!

SUICIDE

WHY WAS IT—OK

for me . . . to want to end my life;
for you . . . not to care if I did;
for you . . . to let me die;
for you . . . to let me slip away;
for you . . . to leave me alone;
for you . . . to want to kill me;
for you . . . to give me no hope;
for you . . . to lose your hold on me;
for you . . . to let me go;
for you . . . to destroy me;
for you . . . to suck the life out of me;
for you . . . to destroy my spirit;
for you . . . to take my life;
for you . . . not to give me breath.

for you . . . why . . . why was it—ok . . .
for me . . . why . . . why was it—ok . . . to still love you . . .

HOW COULD I PERMIT THESE THINGS?

I died alone each and every day.

Then I had those days when I just simply wanted to kill myself. I will never know what stopped me. I don't know what took my hand from me. I don't know whether I was cursed or spared. I only know that living was the hardest thing I ever had to do.

I had a haunting desire to die. There seemed only light in death. There was only dark in the living.

I attempted a list once of the things I would miss if I were to die. There was nothing on it. Seems silly doesn't it? A list with nothing on it! But it was my truth; it was my existence.

Even sadder, I prayed to God for Him to take me, I begged Him. I pleaded and wept for Him to take me. I wanted to die and I couldn't; not either by His hand or mine. I couldn't stand it.

I couldn't die so I lived as if I were dead; vanishing. The thoughts of suicide lay lingering in me. It seemed not to matter to any one that I was alive; that I had life in me.

The only life I had was to love others. I listened for hours to their weepings. I tended to them, cared for them. I worked hard to heal their wounds; mend their lives. But none of that mattered.

Nothing ever seeded in them. The only love they had for me was the love I had for them. That's all. I was left empty from their taking. I was left empty from my wanting. They only loved my love for them; not me. They had no lasting love for me

You would never stay with me so I offered you burnt offerings knowing you would leave me. I gave you many other things to look at other than me; the IT in me. I gave you other things to hate other than what lied beneath me. I handed you your freedom. I gave you a way out through the other sins in me.

I gave you a way out so you didn't have to love me.

Leave me alone now.

For I just wanted to die!

Know the minds of your children!
Feel the hearts of your children!
Keep sacred the flesh of your child!
Pay attention to each ones soul!!!

BOUNDARIES

WHY WAS IT—OK

for you . . . to take me as your all;
for you . . . to treat me as I were nothing;
for you . . . to take charge of my future;
for you . . . to expect my everything;
for you . . . to keep only the best in me;
for you . . . to throw out the rest of me;
for you . . . to decide without me;
for you . . . to divide us;
for you . . . to trap me;
for you . . . to take my choices from me;
for you . . . not to allow my decisions;
for you . . . to play God with my life;
for you . . . to take all authority;
for you . . . not to allow my journey;
for you . . . to control my destiny;
for you . . . to paralyze me;
for you . . . not to let me move freely;
for you . . . to make demands of me;
for you . . . to be free to be;
for you . . . to take my freedom from me;
for you . . . to push me;
for you . . . to talk down to me;
for you . . . to diminish me;
for you . . . to weaken me;
for you . . . to refute my mind;
for you . . . not to praise my wisdom;

for you . . . to move my will;
for you . . . to shift my stance;
for you . . . to alter my values;
for you . . . to dismiss my ideas;
for you . . . to shut my mouth;
for you . . . to force my path;
for you . . . to stir so much chaos;
for you . . . to cause such destruction;
for you . . . not to fight for me;
for you . . . to reign over me;
for you . . . to be my authority;
for you . . . not to be accountable;
for you . . . to hold me accountable;
for you . . . to be so selfish;
for you . . . to expect me to be selfless;
for you . . . to sit in judgment of me;
for you . . . to behave as if you were God.

for you . . . why . . . why was it—ok . . .
for me . . . why . . . why was it—ok . . . to still love you . . .

HOW COULD I PERMIT THESE THINGS?

My heart was on fire. My fire was no match for the steel in your souls. You were ice cold. No thaw of mine could penetrate you nor melt you.

I saw everyone's pain. I felt everyone's pain. I acknowledged everyone's pain. I heard everyone's cries. I neither saw, felt, acknowledged, nor heard anything for my own soul. I lived for you. You never tended to me.

So I searched for my own strength. With each step of strength I took, the weaker you wanted me to be. The harder you slapped me down.

The more flames I had for you the colder you became. When I made shifts in my life in order to survive the more furious you became with me.

I wanted you to stay with me, so I conformed to your will.

I grew no boundaries of my own; except to never get too close to anyone; for they would leave me if they saw what was inside.

I knew the difference between right and wrong.

I knew the difference between what was just and what was unjust.

I knew the difference between what was fair and what was not fair.

I knew the difference between truth and lies.

I knew the difference between secrets and privacy.

I knew the difference between love and hate.

How could they not. Was I all alone? I could not understand.

So I settled for what I knew, the least of all these from you; the injustice, the unfairness, the lies, the secrets, the hate. I took it all.

Strangers were kinder to me then you were. But I loved you anyway.

What are boundaries anyway? Four walls? Confinement? I had been there in that basement; trapped. I could not say no! I had to say yes. There was only one choice and that was to please. I knew I would be safe if I pleased. I did not know what the alternative might bring. So I lived in my tomb. Besides, for a brief period of time I was not neglected. Someone was paying attention to me.

I learned there, your will be done, behind those four walls. I had no will of my own.

So why did I need boundaries? Nothing was ever about me. Life was all about pleasing others; serving them. Pleasing others was the only proof I had that I lived amongst them. For any act of kindness from them only meant they wanted my sex.

I was always picked at. Like a bird; pecking at me. They plucked away my good parts, took them for their own. The rest of me was a carcass. Dead. Loyalty? Devotion? What were these things that remained in me?

Nothing belonged to me, certainly not my heart. When they were done with me nothing was mine, not even my incest. Nothing was mine;

not my words,

not my thoughts,

not my feelings,

not my moments,

not my drinking,

not my food,

not my needs,

not my company,

not my belongings,

not my money,

not my animals,

not my relationships,

not my past,

not my history . . .

I owned nothing. Everything was stripped from me; my works, my dreams, my goals, my soul. It all went into you. You even fought my compassion.

My only motive was to love and be loved. Everything I touched either turned from me or on me. There was a disease in me. You called it possessed. I refused to go there, for I would join with you if I did.

Yes, I do have a disease.

It is called incest. And yes, IT did possess me!

I went trusting; trusting I belonged to you. Trusting as I did behind those four walls, in that basement. Trusting you would care for me. Trusting you would keep me.

I was as a child.

Rest. Peace. There was no such thing in my life. There was no calm in me. There were no streams, no brooks in me; only raging waters. There was nothing to stop the tsunami in me; the gnashing of my soul.

I let it all in; the boards, the bricks, the stones, the rocks, the waste, the contamination, the fierce destruction; the rolling rage of your waters. There was no escaping. You suffocated the life out of me.

I loved you. You never loved me back. I kept waiting; trusting; believing. But your willingness to love me never came. I had no value to you once you had taken my good. You had no willingness to love me; certainly not the rest of me after you took the best of me. I was only worth your hate; after you loved me but for a while.

I still loved you despite your destruction of me. I still wanted to be with you. Hate was better than nothing; at least it was a feeling.

This must be the definition of insanity; to love and never to be loved! I did feel crazy inside at times. I just wanted to be loved. If that is insanity, then I guess I am insane.

I was proclaimed to be insane once, by them. It was always my fault. I was going to be locked up. They were committed to committing me. Funny though, their proclamation became my window of freedom. So I fled. I went out into the world to find true love.

Love always started with still waters, a resting place as a brook or stream. It always ended though as a raging sea. It always ended in what lied beneath. The wrath in you. The wrath in me. Two broken souls.

I seemed gifted though. I had control over my raging; they did not. I was taught at a very young age never to get angry. I guess they were not. Their rage was visible, mine was not. Mine took me privately; bit by bit; piece by piece. Just maybe they came into my life so I could see the rage in me.

None the less, I was still scared and needed to be held. I needed calm.

I lived most of my life so scared to speak. So scared to reveal myself; tell people who I was. So many times, I wished I even knew. With every passing year I became a little bit braver. I revealed the all of me as I knew it at that moment.

My truth only gave them weapons to use against me.

Why was I attracted to the hard-hearted? Why did only the cold-hearted seek me? Where were the tender-hearted?

I pressed on though believing, believing someday . . . real love would come.

Still, I wait.

I found this card many years ago and it inspired me. It gave me courage. There is no author attached to the words. It said this, "And the day came when the risk to remain tight in a bud was more painful than the risk it took to blossom."

So I will keep blooming and get out of this crawl space.

One day, when I grow up, I will be a bed of roses; and there will be no more thorns.

ANGER

WHY WAS IT—OK

for you . . . to spit on me;
for you . . . to bruise my body;
for you . . . to abuse me;
for you . . . to make me afraid;
for you . . . to speak against me;
for you . . . to hold me captive;
for you . . . to instill fear in me;
for you . . . to spill your rage on me;
for you . . . not to be disciplined;
for you . . . not to speak calmly with me;
for you . . . to speak harshly to me;
for you . . . to rage at me;
for you . . . not to warn me of the danger I was in;
for you . . . to disquiet me;
for you . . . to put me in danger;
for you . . . to contradict my every word;
for you . . . to go against me;
for you . . . to claim my peace;
for you . . . not to surrender yours.

for you . . . why . . . why was it—ok . . .
for me . . . why . . . why was it—ok . . . to still love you . . .

HOW COULD I PERMIT THESE THINGS?

You raged at me and I was so afraid.

It was like looking in a mirror. For their anger was what I saw in me. I had been cast out and as alone as they were. So how could I leave them? How could I abandon this me I saw in them!

Anger was a sin, or so I was taught. But really anger is like a tea kettle. It slowly simmers then boils and whistles out loud. Unattended, it spews into rage. It makes itself known. It emits vapor and a constant heat in the air, a steaming. Only a hand can lift this pot from the scorching heat; stop that kettle from boiling and raging.

So too, my life. I needed someone to lift me up and stop the boiling in me.

My anger was not like theirs. It was quiet and private. I did not even know it existed. My anger was still; like an unlit kettle of water. To be angry was wrong; sinful even.

So I took what was in me out in other ways. I became a rebel. I was fiercely rebellious. I was rebellious against all that had come against me and a rebel for anything that needed my help. I fought for every injustice. That was how I raged. I raged in peace. I raged for causes.

There was a wildfire in me.

I was mad inside. I raged myself out of the womb; for I was not to be born. Silently, I raged through the incest. I had no voice, not then, not ever. No one heard the *whispers* of my voice. No one loved the calm in me. So I found causes outside myself. I found soldiers to stand beside me. But that was it, to stand beside me. There was no one to lay with me and stay by my side.

I was cast out. I was cast out from everything that ever seemed to have purpose to me. I was cast out from him. I was cast out from family. I was cast out from friends. I was cast out from church. I was cast out from faith. I was cast out from God, according to them. I was all alone. I was all alone and sadly, angry.

All I took shelter in, was stripped away from me; stripped from me.

I was now homeless.

So I sought other fathers and mothers, brothers and sisters. I sought to build a family of my own. I was cheated out of mine. They lived happily ever after while I lived alone in dread of each and every day with no one by my side.

I lived in fear. I had no fortress as they did. I did not even have them as they stood united; together.

They sat me in the judgment seat of my own innocence. And I bought their sentence upon me. So I lived in dark places. I lived in cellars. I lived in basements. But I was still mad. I was seething with rage. But there was no way out. I was trapped.

Fear is what kept me clinging to this so called love. The fear that they will leave me. So I did everything and anything to keep them. I so desperately put my security in their fleeting good, believing it was love for me. I was afraid to leave that little bit of love. It was better than nothing. At least this was something. I could not live without anything at all. I did not want to live alone, lonely. That hate, their hate was better than the loneliness. My love strings became a web of fear.

I was reprimanded for sins I never committed. But I was never saved from the sins committed against me. I was cheated out of any chance, for any semblance of a normal life. I was cheated out of a life with the living and loving relationships.

If I had only known I was so splintered; so young and splintered. Everything was distorted. I looked at life fragmented. There were no rose colored glasses, only shattered lenses. I could see nothing. I could only feel the pricks of the splinters. And they hurt. And I could not free myself from them. They were embedded in me. They pricked the wrath in me. The wrath I wanted out of me.

How dare you do these things when I could not fight; when I did not know I even needed to fight! I did not know that I was in danger.

I was blamed for their evil; their dark side. This was not me. I believed in love and to do good. I violated no one. But according to their standards, even my good was evil. It was their way to control me and make me theirs and to hold me in their fold.

I was cast out of holy places because I was evil; them knowing IT was evil; the incest. Judging me, condemning me took away from the truth. Condemning me was far easier than dealing with the truth.

The casting out of me was only one loss. The truth would have many casualties. The sacrifice of one was far easier than the death of many.

I lived a life with those of double sided mouths and double sided hearts; hypocrites. You hypocrites with your cold and calculating hearts speaking in soft words and you hypocrites that raged at me while claiming to love me. Hypocrites—only Sayers, never doers; while claiming to love me!

You sit on your throne and point your finger at me. You throw your stones at me. You don't even know me.

You don't even know who I am.
Yes, I am scared! Of you!
Yes, I want to rage! At you!
Yes, I am so very angry! With you!
Yes, I am mad!
You don't even know who I am.
And my heart is broken.

ADDICTION

WHY WAS IT—OK

for you . . . to practice yours;
for you . . . not forgive me of mine;
for you . . . to be tolerant of yours;
for you . . . not to be patient with mine;
for you . . . not to believe in me.

for you . . . why . . . why was it—ok . . .
for me . . . why . . . why was it—ok . . . to still love you . . .

HOW COULD I PERMIT THESE THINGS?

I quit rocking when I started drinking. Rocking was for children. Now I swung hand to mouth.

I drank so I could not feel my flesh. I never knew my flesh to be my own. I could never attach my flesh to my soul. They were never one.

Incest. It's like being convicted of a crime that you did not commit and being imprisoned for years. Alcohol freed me from those prison bars. I could suck down the rage and numb the pain. So I went in behind other bars.

The times that I was sober I became a third person. I was a foreigner within my own body. I only seemed alive because of my spirit but I did not know who owned my body. It was separate from me. It did not belong to me. I hovered over it but I did not live there. I couldn't mingle with it. I was just there but where? I knew those around me but I didn't know this other; that flesh called me.

I was immensely sad when I was sober. It was agonizing. I was always on the verge of tears and my heart so desperately ached. I was detached and had no belonging. Alcohol helped me maintain this sense of detachment so with its help, I got really good at separating myself from the living. It was so familiar to me. I knew it. I knew the pain. The loneliness was home to me. I could survive there. It could fill my empty holes. Alcohol became my best friend. I could depend on it. It kept me stable. Without it, if I were not so sad, I felt a well of rage and such a strong desire to punch someone out; me. I needed to scream. Alcohol stilled my voice. I was either sad or mad so I kept drinking.

Every aspect of my soul was gone. Lost. Stolen. Whatever fragments I could hang onto, I did my best to hide them from harm. It was the best thing, the only thing, I knew to do.

My addiction helped me to play. My addiction allowed me to have fun. My addiction was playtime for me, child's play. That lost innocence.

My addiction also held me back. It held me back from being a force to be reckoned with. It kept me meek and closed my eyes so I could not see. This too I knew and learned from my beginnings.

My heart shriveled up. I longed to love but no one would love me. My alcohol embraced me. Wrapped its arms around me and held me. It stayed with me. It stayed with me through everything. It never left me. It never rejected nor abandoned me. It never judged me. It accepted me. It did not leave me alone nor did it forsake me. I could depend on it. It let me be me. It did not force me to do anything I did not want to do. We were partners in life.

What relationships I had in life offered nothing, yet I felt so in love. They were void, empty and gave nothing. Maybe romance in the beginning. But love never remained. I was nothing to them once the romance was over. Just like I became nothing once the act of subtle incest was over; that quiet nothing. The physical tender touch of another human being by your side then the heart lays lying alone; so too my alcohol. I learned quickly to live without the human touch and to keep my heart lying alone.

I became a master of my own craft. The craft of pleasing. Nothing in return. This splinter grew deep in me; perhaps deeper than all the rest. I don't know for sure. What I do know is that it became my fortress. It kept me in the darkness I was familiar with. It shielded me from all the other splinters in my soul; those splinters that were growing into thorns. They quietly grew in me. I watered them as one would water a flower.

Alcohol became this magic potion. It validated me. It kept my soul in its place; away from me. I tucked it in to be my greater force. It was my sword against the living. It kept me in a hiding place; a safe place. It became my defender. It protected me. It kept me in the dark, down in a safe place. It became my basement. It was the only sword I had to keep you from me. It shielded me from your arrows.

I could not be touched. I could not be betrayed. I made sure no one would want me. No one could do me harm there. I was detached. My splinters may puss up but I could pluck them out there. They could no longer grow to thorns. They could no longer seek refuge in me. I was gone. I was out of here. Gone. Plant your thorns in someone else for I do not feel a thing.

Go away all you liars!

Go away all you hateful people!

Go away all you who cast judgment on me!

Go away all you who use me!

Go away all you pretenders!

Go away all you church goers!

Go away all you hypocrites!

Go away all you cheaters of my soul!

Go away all you who leave me!

Go away all you righteous ones!

Go away all you stone throwers!

Go away all you Pharisees!

Go away all you naysayers!

Go away all you who never had to live in a basement!

Go away all you who never had a basement you could not get out of.

Leave me alone so I can live in this hell all by myself.

I was warned against alcohol and other addictions but I did not trust those who spoke against them. After all they were evildoers of their own kind.

Addiction was prophesied to me before I ever took my first drink. I was accused in my innocence. I was accused of taking stronger drugs. I was innocent. So I gave them a way out for those who were guilty to put me away. So I could be vanished.

Alcohol was the only thing I owned. It belonged to me. Unlike so many other things in my life, it was the one thing I had a choice in; a say so over. It was the one thing I controlled. I owned it. I claimed it. It was mine. No one could take it from me. I gave birth to it. It was my child. I nurtured it. I raised it. It was the only thing that remained. It permitted me to vanish just as they desired.

Alcohol loved me. It was my savior. It was my constant companion. It would stay by my side forever. I trusted it. It was consistent. It was my safe place. I could not be found there. I could be lost and not found. I knew this place. It was where I resided. It was where I laid—waiting—waiting to be saved.

The day came when I wanted so desperately to get out of my own self-induced prison; walking on death row. I did not know how. I came so close to death's door so many times. I did not trust myself. Certainly, I did not trust them, those who had led me here from my beginning. I could never trust them—that land of lack.

I was scared to come alive. I knew my heart, though weak, was still intact. I knew I would only feel for them; as I felt for him. I would only care for them and their lost souls. I would only want to fix all that was wrong; all that was broken. In doing so, I would lose those tiny glimpses of myself. I could not do it. I would lose whatever fragments I had of me.

To love meant to please others. It had nothing to do with me. It began in that basement—I learned how to please. I mastered that craft.

I did not get that I was a child. I did not get that there was this disconnect once this happened. I did not get that I could never develop as a child should. In heartfelt love instead of this physical longing.

I had no understanding that what happened back then was wrong. It just was. It was love to me. It was gentle and kind. The touch drew me in. The sense of touch. I never knew it before not even as an infant. It was calming. I then craved it. For the first time, someone wanted to touch me. I was one with another. I was drawn out of the depths of despair. Someone wanted me. Someone wanted to touch me.

Then he was gone; vanished.

I then was forced to find another to please; some other who would touch me. This one would fill my longing. I thought it would be forever. After all I did such a good job. Forever never came. And he went away too.

So I sought another and then another and yet another. I did it all for nothing. Alone again; aching; longing. Longing to be loved. Aching to be touched. I did it all for nothing in return!

Then there was alcohol. We bonded—we laughed together, we played together, we quietly raged together, we talked with each other, we reasoned together, we laid with each other, we woke up together, we ate together, we drove together, we made choices together, we decided together, we confided in each other, we made love together. It was a perfect union. It stayed. I stayed. It was relentless in holding onto me. Can you imagine . . . the passion between us!

I had visions of wanting to part from it, that alcohol; separate myself from it. Funny isn't it that alcohol was the only thing that I ever wanted to leave me; I never wanted you to leave me. It was the only thing I ever wanted to live without; I never wanted to live without you. I wanted to run from it; not like my needing to run from you.

How would I live with you if I gave up my drinking? Alcohol became my home; unlike the home you threw me out of. How could I quit and find a home? It is so complex, so confusing and dear God—it would take trust.

Trust was something I knew nothing about; the building, uplifting trust. I only could trust those splinters and thorns. If I quit, I trusted they would be back and that they would prick yet even deeper in me. Those infectious splinters and blood craving thorns; they carved a curse in me. The curse of my drinking loved me, you did not.

So I chose it.

The lifting of my hand to mouth with such consistency was like the rhythm of my rocking. It was movement. Drinking took the place of my rocking. My arm constantly swayed to my lips and I drank it down. Oceans of it. And at the end of each day it put me to sleep; just as my rocking did when I was a child, and that banging of my head.

As I grew, I sensed a killing in me so I gave up the hard stuff. I only drank beer now. I knew that alcohol had me, and no, I was not trying to fool myself; beer is alcohol too. But this form of alcohol was more manageable to me. It never snuck up on me and I could still rock, hand to mouth.

I struggled with my addiction to beer. My addiction woke me up every morning and socked me in the face each and every day. But it was always on my mind. Every minute was a battle. For years I thought of little else. When could I have my next beer! My world evolved around it. It became a part of my every decision. It became a part of every movement I made. I could not move. I could only rock.

I hated my addiction. I fought as much against it as I longed to be with it. I eventually tested this battle. I isolated myself with my addiction to see who would win. Who would live and who would die.

I purposely took vacations to see if I would survive alone with all my beer drinking. It did not matter one way or the other to me. I couldn't live anyway.

I bought my first house all on my own. Yes I could work; I could still function. I just could not move. I took yet another one of these weeks off in order to test myself to see if I could live through it. The times before, yes I survived. I survived like a sluggard, crawling on the ground.

This time as I slept one night, I saw this blinking light. It grew in steadfastness and became so bright. There was LIGHT. I was embraced in absolute peace. I had no earthly identity. It held me there for a while then the light began to flicker and dwindle away from me. I fought to stay in it. I fought with all my might to stay in that LIGHT. No—don't push me back! It did. Please let me stay! It did not.

Back on this earth, my brain and my being were euphoric for days afterward.

Yet I kept drinking my beer. This seemed my higher power.

It became even harder to live after that night I died into the LIGHT. Something was different in me now. I felt a deserving in me.

I longed for and ached for sobriety. I had glimpses of what it was like the few times I was able to experience it. Then this shadow would come over me and I would become fearful. What if no one will be there for me in my sobriety? What if no one would be there at the end of my tunnel? I knew what it was like as a child; that absolute aloneness, that absolute loneliness. It was far worse than me being alone with my beer; far, far worse.

I remember back before my twenties I so desperately wanted to have a baby, and I mean desperately. Having a baby would mean I would have to give up my drinking. I would love it enough to give up my drinking in order to have it. I wanted someone to love and not leave me. I wanted someone to cling to and someone to cling to me. I wanted someone to love me. I wanted someone to accept my love. I wanted someone to love me in return. It would have to! But as this desire weaned, I filled my belly with yet another beer.

As I look back, all I ever wanted was that child in me, unknown to me!

I hid myself in bars. I disappeared. I made myself invisible just as they were. The ones that claimed to love me but when I reached out they were not there. Living in the bars was like living with them; just like them; like reaching out to the dead. There was a big difference though, these dead didn't judge me. For they were sinners just like me.

It hurt so bad inside me. I drank the pain. It only looked like I was having fun there in those bars. For no one could see my soul there; not even me.

Beer was food for my soul and food for my body. I could barely eat anything. It fed me and filled me up. To eat would be a sign of caring for me. To eat would be the nurturing of me. I knew nothing about that. It almost seemed evil to me; to nurture one's self.

My stomach would well up when I put food into my mouth. I could hardly get it down. But I knew I had to. So I would force some food down; selective in what I ate. I didn't have an eating disorder but there was something about the mouth. Mostly though, beer filled my belly. It helped me feel full.

Even as a child I could hardly eat. I liked almost nothing. I would sit at the table and force food into my mouth then secretly hide it in my napkin. So many times I rejected the meal on the table. I would get up and fix something else for myself; maybe some toast. Now, that I could swallow.

I would say every day, "I am going to give it up". But that was when I could not drink. I could never say it or do it when I was free to drink. I could only say it at the end of my drinking but I could never do it at the beginning of it. But I functioned like a robot, dutifully. In fact, at home I could not do my duties without it. Once again, doing duties at home meant I caring for myself. Caring for me would mean an acknowledgment of my existence. That could not happen.

I kept reaching to pull myself up. For some time I worked out relentlessly, alone. I ran. I formed teams and organized sporting events; basketball, softball, football. I tried so hard and fought so hard to become a part of life. I wanted life to become a part of me.

I remember one night in the Highlands of Atlanta this horrific fight. I had to get out from my place from yet another bad day. So

I went out into the bitter cold, walking. I walked and walked and walked. I hated what was in me. I wanted it out of me. I wanted it to stop. As always, I talked and talked to myself about it. This time I was raging inside. I was in the cold raging. I was in the cold weeping.

My spirit was dead.

My spirit desired life.

Even my animals wanted me alive in order to be with them. They hated every drop I drank. And I knew it. I saw it in them each time I opened my first beer. They began to retreat. I was fully aware of the affects of my drinking not only to myself but to all movement of life around me. Every living cell was affected by my drinking and infected by my drinking. Even the dead ones.

All became victims to this splinter in my soul. I could not contain this one. This one had me crawling like a snake. This one wanted me in its snares. This one was like a serpent. This one's fangs would devour me should I get up and dare move. So I laid in silence in that dirt, the land of waste, the land below; that solid ground of dirt.

Being alone was frightening to me. Alone sober. I would tremble because it was so lonely without alcohol. I felt like I would fall to pieces. Like a puzzle, the pieces of my life only seemed to come together when I was drinking. Without it, the pieces of my life were scattered; nothing fit.

I asked for strength in my mind. I asked for strength in my body. I asked for strength in my emotions. I asked for strength in my soul. So I could give up drinking.

I made notes about my addiction for many years and about my relationships; most all of them were addicts too. 1992—I wrote to one. "Ignore my pain . . . you are starving; no matter how much I feed you, it will never be enough . . . Well, my plate is now empty; licked clean by you. The next buffet I prepare will be for me. I will feed myself, love and nurture myself. I went to the well with you and you did not drink with me. I wallowed in your darkness . . . but now I am pulling myself up . . . climbing . . . I can see the light, feel the warmth. I am feeling peace. I can crack a smile."

In the same note I wrote, "If I show you my dark side will you stay by my side? And if I opened my heart to you and show you my weakness what would you do?"

My personal notes continued. "If you let someone into your heart, they are going to know your secrets; the privates of your life. If one truly loves you, knowing; then that one must cover you in love. Not harm you, nor hold it against you. That one will protect you, shield you. And stand by your side."

I also wrote something I titled "Valley of Death". It goes, "I read this verse today about giving strong drink to one who is ready to pass away and to give 'wine' to one who is broken hearted and bitter. And to permit one to drink to help one forget one's lack. And it is ok to drink, to no longer remember ones needs or to no longer dwell on one's misery."

I wrote, "Wow, how profound for someone who has spent nearly forty years doing just this. I became tearful. My gut sunk in and I was no longer heavy. A sense of shame left me. I felt a forgiveness come over me; a forgiveness for all my wasted years of drinking my life away. A release came over my body from the inside out. Does this mean I was justified? Justified for all my pain; for my addiction?"

I wrote, "I have been merciless; absolutely merciless on myself for the toll my drinking has taken on my life. I beat myself up almost every minute of every day. My thoughts about myself became far worse than even the act of drinking itself. I was killing myself with self condemnation; a cold heart of self hate."

I wrote, "I felt a melting away of these things upon studying these verses I read. I felt such a sense of forgiveness. I felt comfort. I could hold my child and whisper 'It's OK. I love you."

I wrote, "Suddenly, all my wasted years might have had some purpose. Maybe, I could put some reason to this self destruction of my soul, self destruction of my mind, self destruction of my body, self destruction of my spirit; this behavior I have practiced for all these years."

I wrote, "This addiction of mine did drop me to my knees. Oddly, I began to rejoice in the 'bones' that had been broken in me. I started to be grateful I was still alive after all these years. I was grateful I was able to at least function all this time. I was grateful for the fire in my soul and that I will one day finally end this thing; this addiction of mine."

I wrote, "Now, instead of beating myself to death for the progress I had yet to make, I began to say thank you for the huge progress I had already made; for how far I had come. Now instead of wallowing down there in circles I could pick myself up and help myself crawl out of this pit. I may have a ways to go but at least I have begun."

I wrote, "I worked diligently to change the words in my head from condemnation to gratitude for each and every little bit of progress I made; never forgetting each step I left behind."

I wrote, "I can't help but think that this, this side of my life just too may have a purpose. After all, I Know! I know the shadow of darkness that followed me. I know because I held the hand of death each and every day. I know the haunting of not living life. I know the stillness. I slept with loneliness each waking hour of every day (and in my sleep). I was a part of nothing. I was separate from every one. I was full of emptiness—nothing."

I wrote, "All these things were so familiar to me. I was home here. It was almost comfortable to me. After all, I really didn't know anything else. This was all I knew as a child. I did not understand. My normal self seemed so different from the rest of the world around me. I watched the children play when I was yet a child. As a child, I watched the children laugh. As a child, I watched the children have fun. At times I might join in but I was never really there."

I wrote, "As I grew older this sense of absence grew with me. I was innocent as a child and naïve to my condition; the incest. As I grew older I thought I would gain clarity but it only led to greater confusion. The splinters grew deeper. I thought as I grew older I could fix this difference between myself and the rest of those around me. After all, I had lived longer now, I was a bit wiser, I was able to use my mind. Why could I not figure this out? It should be so simple. I should be able to better manage this life of mine. I was no longer a child. I could stand on my own two feet. I was surviving. Why would my shear agony not end? Why was I still crying so hard within? Why was I still in so much pain? Why did my silent screams never go away?"

I wrote, "I sought fulfillment in my life, with others, but I only found it in alcohol. The pain would fade just as I had faded as a child. I filled my gut till it was so full. I filled my emptiness. I was at home with this numbness."

I wrote, "I began to participate in my own slow suicide. This too was familiar. I didn't care. No one cared. I was robotic now; just moving one foot in front of the other. This was much easier to do; then to feel. This was far less painful than when I was a child. Those days when I felt it all but had nowhere to go, nowhere to run to; I merely wanted to die but did not know why."

I wrote, "I thought that with my drinking I was able to finally join in. I could finally have fun. I finally felt like a kid. I finally was able to play. But as them, these others too did not care; no one cared. The only difference was they were better suited to pretend."

I wrote, "What was wrong with me, in this place called fun? What was wrong with me in this fog I could play in? I found my best friend there. I found my playmate. We played night and day, day and night. I carried it with me. I found a HELPER so I kept it with me. This I was sure of."

I wrote, "I kept aging. I was surely dying. The hole in me kept sinking. I watched as people would look at me and speak. It was as though they were speaking to someone behind me. I was invisible."

I wrote, "My only saving grace was hearing the *whispers* along the way. I heard faint sounds that someone was in there; there was someone inside me. Someone was in there that was good. Someone was in there that helped those in need. Someone was in there that listened well. Someone was in there that had a heart of open hands. Someone was in there who loved too much. Someone was in there that needed love. Who was this someone the world could see? Who was this someone so separate from me?"

I wrote, "I heard the echoes of those around me for many, many years. I heard the echoes of my very own soul. I grew curious about this person within me. I wanted to meet her, to get to know her, just to see; just to see if she was really there. I made a decision to slowly venture inside. I would have to choose life though. I would have to choose life!"

I wrote, "I have now revisited the verse I began with. Now I understand. I first thought the giving of strong drink to someone who is ready to pass away meant to die a physical death. And it was ok to medicate. I now get it; it means to give of strong drink to someone who desires spiritual death."

I wrote, "Drinking separates one's body from one's spirit. One's spirit leaves this earth while the body remains. Drinking, addiction divides one; detaches one from life and the living. Drinking helps one to forget the shedding of one's own blood. Drinking stops the bleeding. Drinking helps one to no longer remember they are in need and to no longer long for things they are missing; the desires of the heart. This is as close to death as it gets!"

I wrote some more, "I then hear a whisper, 'I love you'."

But alcohol was in my breath and in my being. I was red with shame.

Why can I not just stop!!! After all I had quit my smoking; for many years now!!! To stop smoking was extremely hard to do. But I did it. Quit that oral fixation!

I battled for my mind. My heart had been ruined. I so wanted to be sober minded. I can be, when doing mind things. It's duty that trips me up. The everyday responsibilities; I drink to get them done. I hate them. It is another sure sign that I am caring for myself.

I tried and tried to conquer this addiction. I went to meetings a number of times in my life, understanding that they had helped millions of people conquer their alcoholism. But for me it was so sad and depressing. In some meetings I came out wanting a beer more than ever before. This table of people spilling their guts out, revealing their souls yet no one can respond to help them, exchange with them or me. It was like going to confessional only you looked these people in the eye and you saw their bleeding but you could do nothing for them but to hear. Then you send them off out into the world again to fend for themselves with no one to help; with no one to heal them. I bet my life that the lack of love and the lack of help is what brought them to the troth to begin with. It just made no sense to me.

I heard a star once say, in regards to his alcoholism, "It went away so gradually." My God—this was me. There was hope! The star continued, "It got to the point where I couldn't stand the sight, sound or smell of it." Wow, this was how I was evolving; gradually.

I heard a different star say, when he was addressed about his addictions, "Someone has to love me enough to save my life."

Someone just has to love me enough to understand why.

For I am far more complicated than my addiction alone!

THE CREATURES

WHY WAS IT—OK

for you . . . to deny my love for them;
for you . . . to snatch them from me;
for you . . . not to see their souls;
for you . . . not to see their beauty;
for you . . . not to see their beauty at least for me.

for you . . . why . . . why was it—ok . . .
for me . . . why . . . why was it—ok . . . to still love you . . .

HOW COULD I PERMIT THESE THINGS?

Stay!

Yes, they stayed. Unlike you; they stay. They stay with me. They stay with me forever until they are called to a greater home. They knew me better than you did. For that, I know I will see them again, one day. I am sure of that.

I remember each and every one of them; Princess, who was left out in the cold . . . Rusty, who was my shadow; then he was taken from me . . . Coronal, the precious black pup . . . Ben; our lab and Suckey too . . . my Dakota . . . my Phoebe . . . my Zorro . . . The list is long.

I spent my fortunes on them. I fed them before I fed myself. If tithing matters, I did my part and much, much more.

I hate abuse of any kind, but the abuse of animals? This set me off inside!

They depend on our world. I wanted animals since I could remember. I wanted to shield them from harm and loneliness. I wanted them to belong. I picked them up out of boxes and I pulled them out from underneath buildings and from cries at my door in the cold. I saved all I could. It did not matter, the least of their suffering or the most.

I think the greatest by far was this boxer I took in. He was the epitome of man's own evil.

This boxer was in the hands of a drug dealer. He was found with an axe to his head. They put his brains back in and revived him. He became mine. It took a number of years for him to get over his circling and walking around like a dog still on a chain. He had nightmares and would wander unknowingly. This seemed to be the least of it. He cried in pain but yet could not even bark; not speak . . . as I.

I saved another from the pits of despair, out of a cage at a flea market. This one was the one to save and teach the boxer how to be a dog. It was marvelous to witness. If only we would learn from them; to help.

I saw their help for each other. It was a love even greater than mankind had given me. I wanted to join their world. It was real. There was love there.

I wanted to be the guardian of their world. I needed to be. I needed to protect them and give them a home. They were fragments of me and were in need too.

I was tormented with every road kill I saw. I wanted to go after the one that had done this; killed this creature. I was sad and I was outraged.

My torment did not end with the dead ones. The torment was for the living as well. Even the cows in the fields, even the sheep, even the horses even every creature that was bound up; I was tormented. These were the creatures that walked this earth held bound by man.

And you birds who could reach the heavens with your wings; you best not get trapped in our four walls.

I spared the creepers and crawlers and all creatures of the air; even the flies.

I wanted to save them all. It was impossible to hold it all together; to be their god.

Stories of horror; of what man did to them; ripped right through. I did my best not to hear them. The stories of torture brought out the kill in me! I had to avoid them. One got past me though before I could turn it off.

These two boys took a puppy, bound its mouth. This was pure evil; they knew enough to bound its mouth so they would not have to hear the cries of its death. Then they saturated this puppy with, I can't even remember with what; too painful. Turned on the oven, put this puppy in it and let it bake to death. They said the inside of that oven was not even recognizable for all the claw marks; claw marks made by this puppy trying to escape. Trying to get out from the heat of his slow death; this torture.

This was a puppy. These were boys! Whatever made them hate so hard?

I always said, "If I saw a man on the side of the road and an animal on the side of the road, which do you think I would choose to help?" I would choose the animal of course. Man has a choice, they do not.

They are in our hands.

I saw their souls. I saw it in their eyes . . . unlike yours. Theirs was warm and wanting . . . unlike yours. Yours was cold and vacant . . . unlike theirs.

They looked into my eyes and saw me . . . you did not.

They held me . . . you did not.

They kept me warm . . . you did not.

They warned me against danger . . . you did not.

They shielded me . . . you did not.

They kept me from harm's way . . . you did not.

They laid with me . . . you did not.

They protected me . . . you did not.

They wanted me . . . you did not.

They needed me . . . you did not.

They loved me . . . you did not.

They stayed . . . you did not!

I will see them all in Heaven one day!

Will you be there???

INTIMACY

WHY WAS IT—OK

for you . . . to shut off our music;
for you . . . to take your love from us;
for you . . . not to honor me;
for you . . . to forget my truth;
for you . . . to dismiss my past;
for you . . . to ignore my history;
for you . . . to love me conditionally;
for you . . . not to love me unconditionally;
for you . . . to forget our good times;
for you . . . to cheat me of our intimacy;
for you . . . to pretend we were nothing;
for you . . . to forget our conversations;
for you . . . to no longer exchange with me;
for you . . . to erase my words to you;
for you . . . not to be gentle with me;
for you . . . not to give back;
for you . . . to withhold mercy from me;
for you . . . not to weather our storms;
for you . . . to take our "we" from me;
for you . . . to make us all about you;
for you . . . to deny me my imperfections;
for you . . . not to tolerate my weaknesses;
for you . . . to take your warmth from me;
for you . . . to hold back your tenderness;
for you . . . to end the romance;
for you . . . to hold back your touch;

for you . . . to no longer let me touch you;
for you . . . to dim my fire;
for you . . . to refuse me safe harbor;
for you . . . not to hear "I need you";
for you . . . to own me but a while;
for you . . . to dismiss me from now on;
for you . . . to so love yourself;
for you . . . to love me so less;
for you . . . to no longer see my beauty;
for you . . . not to embrace the whole of me.

for you . . . why . . . why was it—ok . . .
for me . . . why . . . why was it—ok . . . to still love you . . .

HOW COULD I PERMIT THESE THINGS?

You never really loved me. You only loved my love for you.

You had no heart so you tried to take mine.

I kept falling for those who only wanted to be served. The selfish; the self-centered. I was the giving one; they were the taking kind. I heard and felt everything about them; about their lives; past present and future. This part was my fault; the listening.

I wanted to repair their brokenness, correct the wrongs done against them, to fix whatever had hurt them. I was kind, compassionate and understanding of their being and of their soul. They loved that part of me.

They loved me in my listening to them, or at least they pretended to. They loved my worshipping of them. That was fine till I needed love back; until I realized I needed them to love me too.

I only knew the servant, pleasing love that my incest had taught me. Nothing was about me. It was all about him, pleasing him. Then the day came when he did not need me anymore; he did not "love" me anymore. What did I do wrong that he left me? What could I do to fix this? Could I have performed better? Would that have made a difference? Would he still be here?

My incest was not an act of violence. It was an act of a child who longed to be loved. The first moments began with gentleness; touching, holding. The final moments were vile and disgusting. Used, betrayed. Those moments of his pleasure cost me my life.

I lived my life believing in those first moments, with those I loved. Trusting, trusting they would remain; unlike him. But like him, if it had to do with me, they left. They sought after their own lives; leaving me behind.

There is no one that really knows me. There is no one that has really stopped to rest a while with me. There is no one who knows my soul. There is no one that knows the spirit that lies within me. I am alone; still waiting.

My idea, my learned perception of love was so distorted. I learned that it was all about the physical world. And that true love was in sexual pleasing.

As a young adult I became obsessed with everything through sexualities' eyes. It was not by choice or in my nature considering my beginnings. The touch I longed for; I could only associate it to sex. I did not know I could be touched without having sex. I did not know I could be held without it ending in sex.

I did not know of the thing in the middle called intimacy.

For a while in my life I so desperately tried to master the final moments of my incest thinking then I could have true love. Someone would then have to love me because they could no longer live without me, without my good sex. Forget about me. They were satisfied. And that was all that mattered. Until . . . I was left alone, again.

Men were not pleasing to me. The scent of them sickened me. It was the stench of their private places. It was the smell of their secret lives. My nostrils flared at them.

So I turned the other direction. I sought after the first moments of my incest. The moments where there was gentleness, tenderness, a longing for me, a desire for me, holding me, touching me. I sought passion this time, with the anticipation of compassion. But still I knew not how to separate sex from love.

I tried loving first, then responding in the physical. I purposely made them wait. I purposely made me wait so I could see a greater side in each of us. We touched on love but only for awhile. Then we had sex and they were gone.

I would move anywhere where I thought love was, with them; and I did. Love—it betrays and blows like the wind. It blows across the country as I did. Love never stays. In the beginning, love believes. In the end love never stays with the believer.

To this day I am programmed in the thinking that any morsel of love is better than no love at all. All of my so called lasting relationships had been abusive. But I kept loving anyway. My love didn't have enough band aids for their wounds and they certainly had no band aids for mine.

In the name of love;

I had knives drawn on me.

I was spit upon.

I was bitten.

I was bruised.

I was beat upon.

I was punched.

I was shoved.

I was slammed against walls.

I was chased down.

I was thrown out.

I was locked in.

These things were the physical.

The first was in the verbal; being told I was worthless; being made fun of; being belittled; being put down. I was called every nasty word out there, so many times, that I then believed in what they said to me.

I could do nothing right, not even love right. The words were worse than the beatings. The bruises healed. The damage to my soul did not. I began to disappear.

I thought I was doing right. I gave up my all for them. I sacrificed everything, all that was me, all that I owned. I thought this would prove my love to them; then they would stay and not hurt me anymore.

Nothing worked.

I was put to shame and publically humiliated with their raging at me. I fought to walk that fine line hoping not to set off their fire cracker should I not behave just right. I walked on razor blades each and every day; every minute of every day.

I had to flee from our first home in order to save my life. I had worked so hard to get it—our first home. It no longer mattered. It was homicide or suicide if I did not get out. I remember my choice as I lay in bed that starry night.

I was then stalked for three years after that great escape. I could not move or breathe. I was scared, constantly. I would fall asleep only to wake up with that someone watching me from my window. I had to leave my place and go to public places in order to feel safe.

I had to call the police, a number of times. I had to put out a warrant. I had hours of tapes with threats to kill me and anyone who dare be with me. Three years of my life ducking and dodging. I was a prisoner again. There was no such thing as freedom.

I could not trust myself in judging relationships; who was for me and who was against me. I could not tell. No one had ever been for me before so I wasn't quite sure how I would know the difference. So I stayed alone.

I stayed alone for some eighteen years. I thought I had given myself enough time to heal; heal from everything. Eventually, I gained some confidence that maybe one day I could try again. I was stronger now and wiser. Or so I thought.

I fell in love with a friend of mine. We had been friends for some fifteen years; "such a guy".

What could go wrong? This was no stranger. We knew many things about each other. We had kindred spirits. We talked for ever about faith, spirituality, relationships, personalities, broken heartedness; you name it. We searched our souls together. We were all but lovers when we were just friends.

Then the day came when we were both single, we crossed that line. I had found that one destined to be with me forever, for the rest of my life. Finally! I had found my protector, my shield, my defender; my wings against the world; my shoulder to lean on. Finally! My prayers were answered; the two shall become one!

I was truly in love for the very first time in my life. This love was real. I surrendered my all.

I gave up the first home that I had ever bought all on my own.

I gave up my job of 21 years. I was going to retire from there.

I gave up most everything I owned.

I went so far as to even surrender a few of my pet angels.

Worst of all, I gave up my family. I had already decided that moving back home would be my next move; then we got together. I know I really hurt them, my family.

I gave up everything and moved states away. I moved under this one's roof in order to be with this one. We would be forever together; or so I thought.

I trusted this one! Our passion was deep; wild. We clung to each other for hours. Apart or together we spoke with each other. We shared our beings.

But now I was in; under this one's roof. Everything changed! I was now under this one's authority. I no longer had any rights.

I became a possession; a piece of furniture. I no longer existed; except for the taking. And when that was used up I was moved to the basement; literally, until I behaved.

Should I not behave me, my animals and what little belongings that remained, would be on the street; literally!

Once again, I was forced to run in order to save my life.

I got what I deserved. Starting at nothing; living above or living below, I deserved nothing.

At the very most, I was below.

There will be no Cinderella ending for me!

RELATIONSHIPS

WHY WAS IT—OK

for you . . . to grind at my heart;
for you . . . not to be fair;
for you . . . to do all the talking;
for you . . . not to listen to me;
for you . . . not to build me up;
for you . . . to dismiss me;
for you . . . to come calling;
for you . . . to hang up;
for you . . . to fear my leaving;
for you . . . to become one that I fear;
for you . . . to control me;
for you . . . not to let me be me;
for you . . . to love my love for you;
for you . . . to no longer love me.

for you . . . why . . . why was it—ok . . .
for me . . . why . . . why was it—ok . . . to still love you . . .

HOW COULD I PERMIT THESE THINGS?

I attached to anything that crawled. They were my kind; the broken, the damaged, the lost, the forsaken, the deceased. They were all alone like me. I loved the crawling so I couldn't love me.

I loved the beasts that walked on all fours so I could not be loved.

There was no chance that someone would love me, someone who was able to soar. Someone who could soar like an eagle or fly like a bird or even flutter as a butterfly. No such one would stop and think to love me. There was no chance of it.

So I lived a crawler's life; a squirming existence. I moved in the dirt and in the dust. At times I had many legs but nowhere to go; as a caterpillar, lost wandering, circling, humping my body but going nowhere.

We crawlers are one. We have no herds. We crawl alone; we crawl alike but never together. We might briefly bump into each other but never did we become one. We take our dust and dirt and crawl on.

Unlike the beasts, there was no herding for us. There was no freedom to roam the prairies; together. There was no companionship that had the four legs it took to run freely, together. There was no standing still and drinking from a stream; together. There was no getting off our feet and gazing at the stars; together. There was no basking in the sunlight to graze; together. There was no mate or herd to surround us; only the company of our dirt.

The birds—they had it all. Birds are free; they have the greatest freedom of all. They live between heaven and earth. It is their moments choosing. They are free to escape this earth's catastrophes; they simply lift up their wings and fly. They fly into the heavens. Where are the birds in this life?

As I crawl, I keep my eye on the sparrow; and long.

Why can I not evolve out of this state of mine?

Why can I not evolve as a caterpillar, to at least a butterfly; they fly too. They may not be sparrows but they do have wings. They live a short while and may not fly high but they do have wings.

I would look up.

I didn't need to be the majesty of an eagle. I just humbly wanted to be a sparrow.

I might have had wings as that of a sparrow. Or maybe even the wings of an eagle. I might have had wings to fly if it weren't for the dark; if it weren't for back then, back there in that basement.

I might have had legs to run the race of life had they not been severed from me; from way back then, down in that basement.

I might have been many great things had my life not been taken from me that day, as a child; that day in the dark.

No wonder there were never any roses in my life.

There were only thorns and thickets.

No beautiful flowers.

No budding to my soul.

Thorns live amongst thorns.

There was no blossoming together.

There is no standing radiant and in full color.

Back In the dark, the seed of death was planted in me.

The decay began.

The petals of my child fell away.

I fade away.

The thorns . . . my only strongholds . . . till dust.

This is how I lived and loved.

The forsaken found me and I found the forsaken.

Who says, love never comes back void?

TRUST

WHY WAS IT—OK

for you . . . to betray me;
for you . . . to conspire against me;
for you . . . to lose interest in me;
for you . . . to have no interest in my life;
for you . . . to speak against me;
for you . . . not to believe in me;
for you . . . to bully me;
for you . . . to change the rules;
for you . . . take back your commitments;
for you . . . to destroy my trust in you;
for you . . . to lie to me;
for you . . . to set me up;
for you . . . to turn on me;
for you . . . not to pick me up;
for you . . . to no longer support me;
for you . . . to threaten my well-being;
for you . . . to steal my refuge;
for you . . . to seize my shelter;
for you . . . to shred my heart;
for you . . . to add a hole to my soul;
for you . . . to pull up anchor;
for you . . . not throwing me a rope;
for you . . . not to quiet my storms;
for you . . . not to comfort me;
for you . . . to let me drowned;
for you . . . to cast me in deep waters;

for you . . . to take your friendship from me;
for you . . . to put me last in your life;
for you . . . to refuse me your arms;
for you . . . to close your outstretched hands;
for you . . . to break your promises;
for you . . . to deny me your once soft place;
for you . . . to break my spirit;
for you . . . to turn away as I lay dying;
for you . . . not to be consistent;
for you . . . to no longer be my rock;
for you . . . to dash my hopes;
for you . . . to remove your stronghold;
for you . . . to snuff out our dreams;
for you . . . not to pull me up;
for you . . . to forget I reached down to you;
for you . . . to lend me helpless;
for you . . . to render me lost;
for you . . . to snatch up my life;
for you . . . not to care for me;
for you . . . not to hold my trust;
for you . . . to betray my confidence;
for you . . . not to respect my privacy;
for you . . . to destroy my person;
for you . . . to erode my confidence;
for you . . . to make a wretch out of me;
for you . . . to shake my security;
for you . . . to alter my compass;
for you . . . to force me to start over again;
for you . . . to take my dreams from me;
for you . . . to instill me with false hope in you;
for you . . . to convince me to believe in you;
for you . . . to create a longing for you;
for you . . . to become my agony;
for you . . . refusing to defend me;
for you . . . not coming to my rescue;

for you . . . not to stand up for me;
for you . . . to no longer protect me;
for you . . . to take your shoulder from me.

for you . . . why . . . why was it—ok . . .
for me . . . why . . . why was it—ok . . . to still love you . . .

HOW COULD I PERMIT THESE THINGS?

You locked me in my room.

I gave you the keys to my heart and you locked me inside.

The keys to my heart were the words out of my mouth. They were truth. I acted in truth. This is where I went wrong. The keys to my heart only unlocked the doors to your hate.

Truth turned you against me; my truth.

As life passed on, I learned to quit passing out my keys; the keys to my heart. I locked the keys to my heart in a tiny little box inside me. No one could get to them; not even me.

I heard about little white lies. I knew they were dangerous; they grew into suffocating vines. I wanted no part of them. So I shut up.

There is a double-sidedness that seeds in one's soul as a result of incest. A deep fog as to what is truly real and what is truly false; what is truth and what is not; which is a lie.

How does one reveal one's self and how does one shield one's self.

I simply wanted to be true. But I trusted no one; my experience had taught me well.

Truth is the neck that lies in the guillotine, just waiting to be chopped off by another one's hand.

Truth is equated to death; death to one's own soul. People bury themselves in lies, in denial, in secrets, in deception, in self preservation. That's how they survive. I wanted no part of it.

I only wanted to be me, as best I understood me, at that moment. I understood enough to know that there is a constant evolving in all things. In my heart I knew in every evolution there must be truth in each of us.

This was the island I stood on, all alone.

They say the truth will set you free. But only if you trust; why could they not handle the truth?

I learned after many swift blows, I had to be careful with my truth. This was hard for me. I always told more far, far more than I ever needed to, to be sure I held no secrets and just in case I might be accused of not telling the truth. But the more I revealed the fiercer the rejection. The more I revealed; the stronger the hate. The more I revealed the more weapons that were used against me.

But I would not lie. So I went into myself and grew silent.

I became a creature, unable to speak. I walked on all fours, following; waiting for any morsel I could get. I waited for any morsel you might throw me; never a plate of food.

I handed myself over to them, surrendering in silence.

I handed myself over to your protection; protection of my heart, protection of my mind, protection of my body, protection of my soul, protection of my future, protection from my past.

I handed the whole of me over to you only to discover I was only protecting you; against me.

I gave you my all; then you gave me no rest.

Your whirlwind was your gift to me.

Truth? . . . love or hate!

Truth? . . . help or harm!

These were my choices.

If you cannot be with me in my valleys, then certainly I do not want you with me on my mountaintops. You either love me or hate me. You either help me or harm me. I trust nothing in the middle.

My life is not a Chess game; nor Monopoly, nor Clue. There are no moves outside of me, there is no money that can buy me, and there is no guessing as to who I am.

But there is no trusting in who you say you are!

Such a fool am I!

DENIAL

WHY WAS IT—OK

for you . . . to promise to love me;
for you . . . not to keep your commitment;
for you . . . to deny me your promises;
for you . . . to take back your forever;
for you . . . to no longer believe in me;
for you . . . to tell me to trust you;
for you . . . to say I could believe you;
for you . . . to give up on us;
for you . . . to no longer share;
for you . . . to stop caring for me;
for you . . . to put me in danger;
for you . . . to cause harm to me;
for you . . . to pretend you loved me.

for you . . . why . . . why was it—ok . . .
for me . . . why . . . why was it—ok . . . to still love you . . .

HOW COULD I PERMIT THESE THINGS?

Your standing was only in your sitting. Sitting down and doing nothing!

Your standing was not on your feet, fighting. But your standing was in your sitting; sitting by and doing nothing! You would not help me!

You could not, nor would not even help yourself. How dare I think you might help me?

Rituals kept it all in check. I learned to master two crafts; first, the craft of the affairs in that basement; the second, the craft of denial.

I mastered the craft of denial from your "conspiracy of silence".

As many in my situation, I have very little memory of ever being a child. I remember great details in that basement. Those moments frozen in time; but I could never tell you how many there were.

Those memories had nothing to do with being a child; innocent. An innocent child with no burdens to bear.

I took on the burdens of the whole world; near and far. I felt so pressed, so squashed down. I felt responsible for all of this world's insanity and for every injustice. But I was just a mere child.

I finally learned how to play though. I learned best how to play all is well.

I learned how to play all is fine.

I learned how to play like nothing was wrong.

I learned how to play this was normal.

I learned how to play this was life.

I learned how to play this was fun.

I learned how to play this was love.

As a child, all I ever wanted was for someone to just simply play with me; to just have fun with me.
Would someone just please come out and play with me?
My only child's play was in playing alone. But I was not there. I was just pretending to be.

I played in pain. I played in confusion. I played haunted.

I played in my imagination; a whole lot. It freed me from reality. Innocence lost!

I just didn't know how to play; child's play!

The day came, one day when I was old enough; that I had to run. I was told I would be locked up for my imperfections. I would be put in prison. Not the prison of legal bars but the prison of institutions. So I mastered yet another, running. I ran from them and tried to run to me. I just wanted to leave me behind. So everywhere I ran to, I was barely there.
I wish I could have left me behind. At times I ran so fast that it almost seemed to work. I had almost left me in a grave behind.
I can't even count the places I have been or the number of moves I have made in my lifetime. Each time I moved I believed in a better life for me. I played like I was all grown up. So here I am in my fifties and right back where I started from. Same town, same body, nothing gained. I have worked hard all my life, but have gained nothing.
There has never been a foundation for me. There has never been anything for me to stand on. There has never been anyone who stayed. I deceived myself, believing they would. He didn't stay so why should they? I needed to be loved in return.

His was so kind and gentle or so it seemed. His seemed to be forever or so I thought. But the only forever that remained was the forever in that basement.

I am still waiting to be loved. I ran and I ran and I ran in order to seek it. Nothing! I ran to my imagination as a child; it was ok there. Then I had to grow up and really run away. I thought I would be running to; running to a life like in my imaginations. At least something then might be real.

I think it's the secrets. The secret keepers; they never free us from bondage nor do they keep us out of harm's way. They had their secrets and then I had mine. I then held the secrets of other children. Their secrets were far worse than mine.

What was done to them as children was unimaginable. I was a child when these secrets were told to me from a child younger than me. These secrets were told to me in the school yard, behind the school near those swing sets.

Back then I could only listen. I had no secret to tell. I had no memory back then of what had happened to me. Even if I had, what happened to them was far, far worse.

Or was it?

Theirs was eventually known.

There were many victims in that house hold; they had each other to talk to, to scream at.

I was just one, alone.

Either way, one or many, surviving is living hell!

Secrets are like dominoes. One touch! One touch is all it takes; that one touch that falls from one generation to the next. The gravity of it! Black squares with white spots. Dark corners with white circles alluding to be light!

If I could just breathe the secrets; give them life. Then maybe I could breathe. Secrets are life's decay. Secrets carry you through life with the stench of death all around you; suffocating you.

You decay ever so slowly and no one even knows; not even you. Secrets open the door to darkness. Secrets isolate you from life. Secrets turn ones soul to ashes.

Then there is the mockery to those who get found out—the victims of incest. Little wonder most won't tell. There is no mercy on those that are found out. They did not tell their secret but their secret was found out.

Is there any mercy on them??? Oh No!!!

These are the ones that become victims all over again, and over and over again. They are set aside for slander. They are set aside for shame. They are mocked. They are neglected. They are put down. They are cast aside. They are pushed away. All by you, because of $|T$.

They are the embarrassment of one's family; the victims of incest.

The cycle goes on. It is the heritage that one owns in the cycle of incest. It is the family decease; some families have cancer. Ours is the disease of incest. A heritage of dark secrets; a heritage under the dim light of $|T$; each of them kills.

I had a thought once that went "Maybe God keeps secrets from secret keepers." Hum. Without truth, there may be treasures that might not find you? Without truth, there may be treasures you might not find? Are there treasures in the truth?

How dare you deny me the truth!

How dare you to agonize me with your silence!

Just because it is my truth does not mean that it is a lie! How dare you!

Where is your truth?

You can hide it from me!
You can never keep it from God!

HERITAGE

WHY WAS IT—OK

for you . . . not to see my pain;
for you . . . not to believe that I love you;
for you . . . not to participate in my life;
for you . . . to cast me out;
for you . . . not to be a part of me;
for you . . . to put conditions on me;
for you . . . not to hear my voice;
for you . . . to make me move;
for you . . . not to see my devotion;
for you . . . to ignore my cries;
for you . . . not to lend to my pleadings;
for you . . . to punish me;
for you . . . not to give me understanding;
for you . . . not to see my innocence;
for you . . . to get on your knees;
for you . . . to be able to rise;
for you . . . not to see I fell on my knees;
for you . . . not to pick me up;
for you . . . to grow me up;
for you . . . to give me no choice;
for you . . . to silence me;
for you . . . to give me no voice;
for you . . . not to be my safe place;
for you . . . to deny me heaven.

for you . . . why . . . why was it—ok . . .
for me . . . why . . . why was it—ok . . . to still love you . . .

HOW COULD I PERMIT THESE THINGS?

93

I could not shake the dust off of my feet, the dust of their curse. I took it with me everywhere I went. I was no longer saved. I went against them. I was no longer fit for their kingdom. I had betrayed their ideals, so I was no longer worthy.

I went against everything in order to find myself. I could no longer cling to them. I would stay in danger if I did. They were not my fortress. They had become my enemy. They only spoke in "Thou shalt not's".

They believed in me but for a while. But that was only because I lived under their law. I had plenty of faith until the gates were locked from me. I quit being this good little church girl. I wanted answers. I developed a fire in me. I had a roaring flame. I guess it matched the fight in me from my birth, only this time I gave it voice. I was no longer a blessing in their eyes. I was their curse.

Christ-like, huh! You took away my faith.

I quit believing after this. Acceptance? Not from them; not from Him. And I believed them! I believed in their hate. I could no longer believe in Him. What God would do such a thing? So I ran to scholars, unlike theirs and searched their "scriptures".

I became the prodigal daughter. I went out; only it was not the gospel I was preaching. I had to hate God for He did not love me. He cast me out. I was taken from Heavens gates. He snatched Himself from me.

He hated me and rejected me for who I was. I was disowned; according to them, separated. I no longer belonged, not to Him nor this family.

I proclaimed Atheism, with my fists held high. If He disowned me; according to them, then I would disown Him; according to my own.

I was taught; judge not lest you be judged.

And the lesson of casting of the first stone; those who have no sin, cast the first stone.

And the beam in your own eye versus the splinter in another's eye.

Whatever happened to these so called truths?

So I went off to another land to seek another family. I left the self righteous. Now they could rejoice. I was their sacrificial lamb. I was their sheep led to their slaughter.

I do not know all their secrets but I certainly carried all their sins and iniquities. They made a little Jesus out of me and crucified me. Believing their secrets would go down with my death. So I died carrying a little Jesus in me as I wandered. I hoped one day, their sins would find them out.

In my own heart, I had never done enough wrong to justify such hate for me. I would take a bullet for them but they would never think to fan a feather for me.

I kept cleansing myself with each and every move. I would buy new clothes, new shoes, more dishes, different appliances, more yard tools, new screws and nails, new shelving's; new nuts and bolts, new light bulbs, new books, new music, new videos, new wall hangings, new bedding; new paint, new candles, new groceries, new everything, as if I had never existed before. I re-birthed myself each and every time.

I started over only to go back to where it all began; home.

I moved maybe thirty times. I moved just to rest my head. It never happened; I could find no peace. I would move again and start all over; over and over and over again. I had a restless spirit knowing I had no belonging.

If only I could do everything over.

If only I could do over my birth.

If only I could do over my incest.

If only I could do over my faith.

If only I could do over the defenses I never had learned.

If only I could do over my childhood.

If only I could do over my bad decisions.

If only I could do over my drinking

If only I could do over my wandering.

. . . if only . . . if only I could do over my life . . .

. . . if only I were never born . . . if only!

I wish I were able to do it all over again; all of it from the very beginning. Maybe I never would have had to live in such confusion. Maybe I never would have had such deep holes in me. Maybe I would have had a soul; a soul that could give without being taken.

Growing up, God's name was on everything. He was in my church, in my school, in the radio at home, all the time; He was in every conversation I ever had with my parents. He was everywhere I breathed. He breathed down my neck. I was raised this way. It was such a narrow path with walls of hate and judgment. There was no room for the seekers of God. There was only room for the righteous. I was not amongst them.

The righteous were too busy shaking their fingers at me to hear a word I ever said; to hear a word He said. Their shaking of their finger was louder than any voice I ever had; or He had. They were like banging drums. I learned to scream inside. It was the only way I could fight their noise.

That's all it was, noise, the sounding brass of your judgment. There was no love. There was no compassion. There was no mercy. There was no kindness. There was no help. There was no caring.

Their only caring was that I become like them; join their fold. Then they would merit in heaven. It was that badge they were after; their key to Heavens gates. They did not care for my soul. But in their eyes, if others could see that I was saved and I walked their walk and talked their talk then they drew closer to the gates of Heaven.

It was all about them. It had little to do with my salvation.

Whatever happened to the words you taught me about this little light of mine? You would not let it shine. You kept blowing on my light; wanting me to vanish, so I would not shame you; because I would not follow you.

You called me possessed. You said I had a demon in me. If this were true then why did you not fight evil with good? You claimed I had evil in me so you fled from me. Oh you of little faith, why did you flee. Why did you not stay by my side and trust God would take care of the rest?

Maybe I lived to close to the truth. Maybe that's why you wanted to put me away.

Jesus was called possessed, too. They said He had a demon in Him. He too was accused for loving others and wanting to be loved.

Don't take my word for it. READ IT!!!

You were scared of my fight. The fight I had in me from birth, the fight I had in me in that basement, the fight I had in me to survive. The passion I had for Jesus; the furious passion in me. The fire of love I had in me. The Love; so, so much love!

I bought into your perfect looking lives. And I longed for them; to be like you and have a forever relationship; your stability; the security of your homes; your wonderful children; your families . . . I coveted it all compared to my shell of nothingness.

By your law, I could never have anything.

I wish I were God sometimes, only so I had the power to show you in numbers the people that have committed suicide, denounced God because you said so; those who fled from your churches and died alone, those who lived broken with not any hope. I could go on. But it was all because of you! I wish I could show you the numbers your sword has severed from God.

You used your rod and your staff against me. You fended me off. I was not the wolf. I was one of your sheep.

Isn't a shepherd to seek his lost sheep; not chasten them from the flock?

Judging was easier work than simply loving.

Those who have had no swords, but have had only swords used against them, will eventually one day gently pick up their own knives only to harm themselves. They will quietly die by their own hands rather than to live with the thrashing of your sword.

I am living proof that all good and evil begins in the home; at home in the Word and at home in that basement.

One is only as cold as one's heart is.

There is evil in the stronghold of cold love. Cold living is the darkest side of life. This is where evil lurks amongst the living; in the cold.

I hated cold weather; or so I thought, but was it really the coldness of their hearts that kept me from home?

I was pushed out into the wilderness by them; chastened.

I did find moments of warmth there in that wilderness; an acceptance of my existence. I finally belonged somewhere. I was welcomed into this world. I saw some angels there. They were kind and generous. They took the time to know me but if even for a while. They loved me and I loved them. There was no hypocrisy.

They were stained and I was stained. We shared our stains and how they got there. We shared our past and how we would live on. We were honest and truthful. We stood imperfect, together. We helped each other.

How was it I had to get out into the world to find help???

I stamped a triangle in me, my one tattoo. It has a message and it is over my heart. It is a dream catcher. There is a triangle in it, pink. And over it is the Cherokee spelling of the word "peace". My initials are there too.

So if one day, if anyone thought I might have existed there, they would now know that I did!

The one sure identity of my remains.

FORGIVENESS

WHY WAS IT—OK

for you . . . not to forgive me;
for you . . . to think you need no forgiveness;
for you . . . to believe you did nothing wrong;
for you . . . to insist it was all my fault;
for you . . . not to apologize;
for you . . . not to accept my apologies;
for you . . . not to see I was on my knees;
for you . . . not to get on your knees;
for you . . . to go on blaming;
for you . . . to keep me begging.

for you . . . why . . . why was it—ok . . .
for me . . . why . . . why was it—ok . . . to still love you . . .

HOW COULD I PERMIT THESE THINGS?

He who forgives least, loves least. This was a proverb I read.

I think I am just beginning to understand a lifelong mystery to me.

I have a lifelong mystery in me. How come all my relationships evolve into abuse? I got beat on over and over again, in every way. I finally hit back once. This was the worst part of it all. I finally became one of them.

I always thought it was because I was not yet perfect. I must try harder so they will stop their beatings of me. After all, I forgave them each and every time, over and over again. Why could they not forgive me just one of my transgressions; at least just one of mine?

You will know ones heart by their level of their forgiving. Those who forgive much; love much. Was my heart really that huge? Were their hearts really that small? Was there nothing inside them? Was there nothing inside me other than the need for them?

I wrestled all my life with the mystery of the turning of one's cheek. I always stayed in abusive relationships. Trust me; I turned far more than my check. I believed I could fix them.

I was given morsels of love just to keep me fed. And I ate. I ate every morsel believing it would satisfy my hunger. The need to be filled. The need to be satisfied. The need to be loved. The need to never have one leave me again. Once in a while, I ate at their tables only to puke. I had no choice but to puke in the end.

I never even thought of forgiving him. I did not know he needed it. Maybe that's been my problem all along; I didn't even know he committed a crime. Innocence; I guess. What happened in that basement was normal; natural even.

But even as I grew I could not grasp the magnitude of the crime against me. And that someday, in some way I would need to forgive that horrible injustice to my life.

Much later still, as some truth was welling up in me; I sought all kinds of excuses for |T and him. He was just a child too. For him to act out on these things, well he had to have learned |T from somewhere. I was sure someone had violated him too.

So I forgave him even before I spoke with him. I forgave him because they said so and it was simple.

But forgiving the one that did |T to him? Now I am raging.

This was the big one. This one was very hard. This one, this was the impossible one. He had taken others along the way in his path of destruction. There is only confession from those who told on him. But others . . . those who dare not speak . . . ???

Does one first have to confess in order for their sins to be forgiven? In this case, of those who remain silent, he never did. He still walks around with a smile on his face!

Oh, the sins of other peoples fathers!

The sin of incest was on both sides of our tribes; the white man and the Indian. We just got stuck in the middle.

Incest is such a norm these days. We as a people deny it; ignore it's detruction.

No one knows the soul beneath; the damage that lies within!

For we are the ones not forgiven!!! We, the incest survivors.

There was no forgiveness for us and how we turned out because of |T.

The perpetrators have all kinds of forgiveness; loving-kindness and tender mercy towards them!

We, the perpetrated are left out on our own, alone, cast out in shame with not even a hint of redemption.

We know the quiet little hate you have inside for us. We feel your invisible whippings and your silent torture toward us.

You apologize for us . . . not to us.

The word forgiveness takes on such a spiritual righteousness when you say you have forgiven. It is such a pretty band aid to the secrets to ones soul. But when you peel it back you see the true festering that lies beneath; like raw meat, yellow with puss.

Saying you forgive meant they got away with it; their violation of you. How do you forgive those who have no remorse? How do you forgive those who blamed only you?

Your act of forgiveness was only for you. It had nothing to do with me. You forgave him not me. What forgiveness did I need? Was it that mirror in your face? Truth??? That mirror in your face when you looked at me? A truth apart from me?

I had to run for my life. There was no time. I had to save myself from them. Forgiveness was not an option. There was no time to even think about it.

How do you forgive someone who never says they are sorry? How can sorry ever undo the damage to one's soul. It is impossible. It just can't be done. It is too huge.

Incest never forgets!

SEXUALITY

WHY WAS IT—OK

for you . . . to take my virgin soul;
for you . . . not to see I was a mere child;
for you . . . to cheat me of my innocence;
for you . . . to take my birth-right;
for you . . . to give me no identity;
for you . . . to hate me;
for you . . . to want my love;
for you . . . to make a wretch out of me;
for you . . . to call me a wretch;
for you . . . to lay me down;
for you . . . not to let me stand;
for you . . . not to hold them accountable;
for you . . . to cast me out;
for you . . . to violate my sex;
for you . . . not to tolerate mine;
for you . . . to offer forgiveness, but not for me;
for you . . . to show mercy, but not for me;
for you . . . not to see their evil;
for you . . . to call me possessed;
for you . . . not to see their perversion;
for you . . . to call me perverted;
for you . . . to warn your children;
for you . . . not to warn them against you.

for you . . . why . . . why was it—ok . . .
for me . . . why . . . why was it—ok . . . to still love you.

HOW COULD I PERMIT THESE THINGS?

I lived with Pride; humbly, differently than your pride. I lived with great Pride as I whispered through life.

I struggled deeply with this chapter. But not to include this part of me would be to hold back an important truth in me. I want no more secrets.

The other struggle I had with this truth was that it would be attached to my incest. It is not. This truth has nothing to do with my incest. But this truth has everything to do with yet an added layer of hate and rejection towards me in my life.

The truth is; I am gay. I am an incest survivor. I am gay. I am an incest survivor and I am gay. One has nothing to do with the other.

This was yet another layer of me; another layer of your hate and rejection towards me. But this one was nothing but sheer hate.

I do not know when my incest started but I did know from kindergarten that I was different. There is a movie called "Prayers for Bobbie" about a gay young man that committed suicide. He was raised in a strict religious household, similar to mine. Near the end of this movie, his mother says that she knew from conception that he was different.

Being gay was certainly not my choice. Who would choose to carry such a heavy burden? Who would choose such hate? I lost everything once I told.

A small voice told me to wait to tell, till I was safe and out of the family home. When I did tell, I lost it all. I lost family. I lost friends. I lost the church. I lost my job.

Forget the damage incest did to me; incest was deep inside. No one could see it. This though, this was what leprosy must be like. I was no longer welcome in your church doors yet I would be fired if I did not go back to church.

The most dreadful loss of all was the loss of my God. I could not be saved if I were gay. Being gay was the greatest sin of all; even murderers had courts to defend them; yes and even the righteous ones might crack their doors to let them in should they repent.

What a tragedy.

This pain I clearly remember. The secret in me was out. I knew this secret in me. I knew this secret in me before I knew the incest in me. The pain of the incest was awakening in me. Still many layers lie buried in me.

But this one, once I spoke this truth; there was no turning back. There was nowhere to hide. There was no taking it back. My life was taken from me. My life was torn from me and all I knew and loved turned on me. All was gone. It was like a tornado, a hurricane, an earthquake, a tsunami; all in one. My life was sheer disaster. Nothing remained! There was nothing left for me to claim.

I wished I could have flipped a switch. Which one; my being gay or my telling that I was? Life would have been kinder if only I was born on the other side; your side. The hurt of losing all I knew was unbearable. I was blinded by pain! I was blinded with pain!

And you say I chose this??? This hate you have for me? This hate society has for me? Being tossed out of your churches? This denying of my faith? This proclamation that God cannot love me??? This sentence that God will not love me? Come on; why would I choose to walk on death row each and every day?

I will give you this and only this.

There are those that like to play in my world. They are the Sodom and Gomorrah type. They love sex and orgies. I do not. They love to play in my world, have fun and sexually please themselves in my world. They make a mockery out of my world. And when they are done, they are free to go. I am not!!! They are free to come back again and visit. I am not!!!

Get out of my yard. Stay out of my yard; you perverts!

I was a saint in my world; a sinner in yours, trying to be straight, like you. My sex was sacred to me except in your world where I tried to be accepted by you. I played in your yard, trying to be straight like you. I wanted to stay so you would love me. But I could not. I could not live a perverted life!

There was no acceptance of me; not in your beds, not in your churches.

I believed in your Trinity till you took it from me. So I claimed a triangle of my own. It was the triangle of those who had suffered before me. It has a color; it is pink.

Hitler handed them out to those like me.

He had triangles—so did you.

He made me keep mine, this pink triangle.

You took yours back; you took your Triangle away from me.

Is your hates equal?

He never claimed to have love in him—you did.

Tragically, we who live behind the pink often die by the pink.

We take our flesh—he took the flesh.

We silence our souls—you take our souls.

We, the gay people have our other colors too. We have our Rainbow flag. Yes, there is a rainbow in each of us; we that are truly gay. We fly it with Pride. Not with your kind of pride and boastfulness. But with a pride, that we are alive and living and doing our best to do well and be kind.

I will never understand why you did not hate my incest as passionately and powerfully as you hated me for being gay. I never took a child!!! Incest is a choice; homosexuality is not!

This may be my sin in your eyes; as you molest your children without sin.

Do you even have any clue as to how many gay children; how many gay people commit suicide because of your hate; because they could never shake the dust off their feet for holding on to your city??? Believing in you? Not understanding they needed to believe in God before you? Not believing they were God's design; believing they were your clay?

You chastened us from God. You drove us away from Him. You drove us to taverns and unwanted places. We just wanted to be loved—merely loved!

"Jesus loves me this I know." So you sing. Keep on with your hate. Take your innocent children and go to your churches as to appear sacred. I would never harm a child as you have.

I walked a Jesus walk. The walk before the cross. The mockery; being spit upon; the bleeding of my heart; the flogging of your hatred; the thorns of judgment. But unlike Him, my resurrection would never come; for I was a daughter of mankind.

Your condemnation seemed somewhat easier than the wounds of my incest. I blamed myself for everything anyway. My homosexuality gave you a way out from those darker truths in you; your sexual misconduct and sexual misconducts that were performed by others.

I wish you had the same clinched fist towards those who took innocent children as the fist you raise at me for being gay. You shake your fists in the wrong direction. Why can't you have the same passionate hatred towards incest as you have towards me for being gay!

I just don't get it! I will never understand!

It is dead wrong! I am here to tell you, you are dead wrong. You are wrong on both counts. You are wrong in what you do to your children and you are wrong in your judgment of me because I am gay.

I experienced God's Light one night; the night I died. Yet another night I wanted to die because of you. After all, you told me I would never make it to heaven. This sin was just too great!

But I saw the LIGHT that night. It was pure. It was perfect. It was bright. It was God.

I lived in Him but for a moment.

Then the Light of His presence began to slip away. The magnitude of His Brightness began to fade away. The purity of His being began to vanish from me. The flashing of His Light grew ever dimmer. I fought. I fought not to come back. It was a furious fight. But in the end, He won. He forced me to come back down to you.

Maybe I lived only to tell you . . . you are dead wrong.

You cast me into the flames of hell. You closed your arms from me. You swore I would never see the light of heaven.

I did.

How is it, God had chosen to shed His Light on me? On me!!! The one you cast out!

You said I would never see the Light of Heaven.

I DID!

I lived in the Light.

You did not!

I know! I saw the Light!

I DID!

And I am still gay.

I carry two triangles now; His, mine—and my Rainbow flag. I carry them all—with Pride!

HATE

WHY WAS IT—OK

for you . . . to no longer love me;
for you . . . to deceive me;
for you . . . to hate me;
for you . . . to give me life;
for you . . . then to take my life;
for you . . . not to see the child of God in me;
for you . . . not to believe;
for you . . . to preach the Word;
for you . . . not to walk in the Word;
for you . . . to become my god;
for you . . . to take my Jesus from me;

for you . . . why . . . why was it—ok . . .
for me . . . why . . . why was it—ok . . . to still love you.

HOW COULD I PERMIT THESE THINGS?

There was no Jesus in you; only the wrath of God!

You took my Jesus from me with all your hate. I wish your passion to love was as powerful and constant as your passionate power to hate.

If only there was no hate in love.

I took your hate and turned it inside me. I turned your hate on me. Your hating me seemed to be the only thing we agreed on. I was not welcomed amongst you unless I became you. So I did join you in your hating of me.

I not only hated me, I hated man, I hated God, I hated the church, I hated society . . . I hated man. You used your sword to divide me from love. So I joined you in your hate so you might love me! I joined you in order to belong! Your contempt was all that I had to hold me.

Hate from you involved turning the other cheek. I had no fists up. I only had love. The only fight in me was to love so I turned my cheek then I turned my other cheek. I sought to love you but there was no love in you so I shook the dust off my feet, the dust of your hate from beneath my feet. I went off from town to town seeking for someone to love me.

The loving of me never happened; for the seed of my worthlessness was planted in me. Its roots were deep in me. The world took my soul. Hate from you! Incest was easy compared to this. At least he never hated me.

It was my deserving by you; by your God. You were on your way to heaven, I was not. I would never go there says you! There was no room for me there. For heaven was only for the righteous. I was not one of them; according to you; according to your laws.

Whatever happened to Jesus?

You searched your scriptures and found ways to hate me. You truly never studied Him, my Jesus. He was the love of my life till you hated Him out of me.

Why were your sins not revealed, oh holy ones. Where were your verses on Lot sleeping with his daughters? You stopped at Sodom and Gomorrah! Whatever happened to your scriptures on Lot getting drunk and sleeping with one of his daughters then the next night, getting drunk again and again sleeping with his other daughter?

I know; now that this is revealed, you are going to blame the daughters!!! I know, I heard it all my life!

Love takes responsibility . . . you did not!

You even preached your hate to me on Father's Day. The one day in all of my entire life I had my father all to myself. The one day just he and I went to church together. The one day in my life I was able to hold him in my hand. The one day in my life he held my hand with pride!

You haters just refuse to let love live; not even for a moment. Not for a moment! Not even for a moment in a lifetime for me and my dad on Fathers' day.

Whatever possessed you to preach a sermon on Sodom and Gomorrah on Father's day? There was no connection. I stared that preacher down. How dare he take my dad from me; that one precious day in my life!

When it was over, my Father wept!

You hid the Words on love; or did you never study them? Your list of sins seemed longer than the Ten Commandments. Did you forget the first? "The greatest of these is love." You hated the sinner and clung to the sin. The sin was your shield to keep you from love! So you could keep your righteousness.

I attended your house of hate all my childhood. I went twice on Sundays and I lived within your laws every single day. I paid close attention to the words taught to me. I searched my own soul for understanding. But there was no one I could talk to or merely ask a question; no one I could go to, to simply seek answers. I dare not after attempting it once or twice. I stayed in my solitude, only to hear you preach.

As you preached each week I learned that so few of us would actually be saved; most all of mankind had been illuminated by you. No one would be saved except we who worshipped there.

I saw every ones suspicions; "are you saved?" I kept looking over my own shoulder.

Would I be next to join those who were not? What might I do to be cast with them; those who where unsaved, those going to hell! It was too much for me to comprehend. I had no one to trust in. For if I spoke, I knew I would be one of them! I knew I would be one of those going to hell!

I loved my Jesus. But He was hidden from me by you. You pounded your chests with the wrath of God. That was your power; the wrath of God. There was no mercy or grace or any of the rest of the fruits of the Spirit.

It was the wrath you wanted me to trust in, live by. Control me with.

This was your faith. This was your religion. The wrath of God!

I was cast out so I had to walk on.

I still loved Jesus and stayed drawn to Him. For some time even, I carried a Crucifix around my neck. I did not know why. I was not a Catholic, nor raised one.

I guess I figured if I hid behind their cross to look at my Jesus, He would not see that it was me. I loved Him and just wanted to be with Him.

I want my Jesus back.

Give me my Jesus back!

I wish you would have hated me loudly so I knew what was happening to me. But you hated me in a still small voice. I had glimpses of the storms inside you; your whirling tornadoes within. You would not fight with me to love. You just slowly shut your doors to me. You would not reveal the storms in you; you would rather hate me. I became your storm. You were quietly vicious towards me.

I wish there was violence in his incest towards me then maybe I would have known it was wrong; then I might have known what was happening to me. Instead, he was gentle and tender and even seemed kind. I was a child then.

I was a child too; when you appeared to love me. Now like you there is a shell of love around me while inside a storm of hate. We seemed to be one now.

You never focused on the beam in your eye. You only focused on the splinter in mine.

I had plenty of them, the splinters . . . and the greatest of these was hate!

I finally belong; I belonged in your hating of me.
I hate for all . . . . that happened.
I hate that you . . . did not love me.
I hate . . . that I still loved you.
I hate for hating me.
I hate hating.
I need you.
I need
!!!!

I need my Jesus back!

Take this cup from me!

. . . shed *Your Light* upon me . . .
. . . and grant me *Your Peace* . . .

. . . for |T is finished!